Bountyfull
Healing

Bountyfull Healing

A Guide for the Broken-Hearted

Larry Mackey, OMI

NOVALIS

© 2004 Novalis, Saint Paul University, Ottawa, Canada

Cover design: Caroline Gagnon
Layout: Caroline Gagnon/Richard Proulx
Cover image: Photodisc, Tancredi J. Bavosi (Getty Images)

Business Office:
Novalis
49 Front Street East, 2nd Floor
Toronto, Ontario, Canada
M5E 1B3

Phone: 1-877-702-7773 or (416) 363-3303
Fax: 1-877-702-7775 or (416) 363-9409
E-mail: cservice@novalis.ca
www.novalis.ca

Library and Archives Canada Cataloguing in Publication

Mackey, Larry
    Bountyfull healing : a guide for the broken-hearted / Larry Mackey.

ISBN 2-89507-524-7

    1. Healing–Religious aspects–Christianity. 2. Spiritual healing.
3. Christian life–Catholic authors. I. Title.

BT732.5.M332 2004   248.8'6   C2004-904287-4

Printed in Canada.

We acknowledge the financial support of the Government of Canada
through the Book Publishing Industry Development Program (BPIDP)
for our publishing activities.

5 4 3 2 1   08 07 06 05 04

Dedication

I dedicate this work to the memory of my mother, Hazel, and especially to my father, Emmett, who inspired me with a love for the great outdoors and for writing.

Acknowledgments

With the publication of this work I would like to acknowledge the support of my Oblate community for providing the facilities at Bountyfull, which has enabled me to carry out my apostolate, and for the freedom they have granted me to develop it in response to the Spirit.

I also owe a debt of gratitude to all the members of our Bountyfull community, past and present, for their dedication and commitment. I would like to acknowledge the Board of Directors, especially Robert Bellows (B.Comm., LL.B.), for their faithful support and guidance since the foundation of Bountyfull. In a special way I offer my personal thanks to Dr. Alan Macdonald, my close friend and mentor who has inspired me in this ministry over the years. In particular I offer my profound thanks to Kathy Stack, for her untiring dedication to the work of typing this manuscript. I am greatly indebted to Patricia Donovan and her community, the Sisters of St. Ann, for their participation in our work, and to Monica Guest and her community, the Sisters of Charity of the Immaculate Conception. Monica's zeal for the poor and the broken helped me to found Bountyfull House originally. Over the years, our Bountyfull community has remained steadfast in its dedication and commitment to the call of the Gospel to heal the broken-hearted and to set prisoners free.

Contents

Introduction

"The kingdom of heaven is like treasure hidden in a field,
which someone found and hid; then in his joy he goes
and sells all that he has and buys that field."

(Matthew 13:44)

Many people wake up every morning in great pain. For some, this pain is due to physical illness, injury or disability. For countless others, there is no physical cause: the pain springs from deep within them, from a hidden, unhealed wound that cannot be detected by X-rays or ultrasounds.

It was this awareness that prompted me, with the approval of my religious order, the Oblates of Mary Immaculate, to found Bountyfull Counselling Society in 1987. For months we looked for an appropriate setting for our new ministry. Through providence and the support of my Oblate community, we opened the doors of Bountyfull House that same year.

Bountyfull House is a sunflower-yellow heritage-style house surrounded by a lawn and shade trees, decorated and furnished to look and feel more like a home than an office. It is located at 530 Heatley Avenue in Vancouver's downtown east side, in what the media calls the western hemisphere's greatest human disaster area. For many it is a haven of hospitality, a safe house in the centre of the storm of drug addiction, the sex trade, and poverty in this, the hardest-hit urban area of the worldwide AIDS epidemic.

Each morning on my way to work, my daily drive down East Hastings reminds me that we are called to help heal the ravages of drugs, alcohol and brokenness that are so prevalent in our world. We see the many homeless and broken people sleeping out on the streets, doing drug deals, or aimlessly milling around. Often our first job in the morning is to don gloves and get tongs to pick up used condoms and syringes from the lawn around the house. These daily realities make the urgency of human healing very meaningful for us at Bountyfull. We are reminded of Christ's words: "The poor you will always have with you." (John 12:8)

At the same time, we find hope in the downtown east side. Bountyfull House is situated in an established part of Vancouver – the Vancouver where immigrants from many nations found a haven of stability many generations ago. Some descendants of the original families are still here today, and their sense of community and friendliness give us energy. Our area has a unique cross-cultural flavour. Older Asian people can be seen practising Tai Chi in the park in the early morning. With his dog Smokie, Joe, the block patron who runs the neighbourhood rooming house, greets all the residents. In the background rings the joyful sound of children's voices from the schoolyard across the street. Daily we witness life and healing springing up eternal in human activity, like the little blades of grass that force their way through the concrete in the sidewalk. We thrill to see how the principle of life, even in such small ways, can break through what seem to be impenetrable obstacles.

Based on our mission of journeying with people who have come to realize that they are powerless, and are ready and willing to seek help, staff members of Bountyfull House listen to the personal life stories of those who seek their support, and then assist them in unearthing the hidden roots of pain and brokenness that bind them. An innovative approach to inner healing focused on the whole person is offered to each in an atmosphere of acceptance and understanding. At the core of this approach are the Bountyfull Principles for Living, which emphasize feelings and unconditional self-acceptance. This work has grown over the years; we now operate with a staff of four. Over the past 17 years we have conducted in-depth counselling sessions for more than 6000 men and women from numerous 12-step programs and from many other walks of life. Through a spiritual awakening, they are able to touch the healing power that lies within themselves and thereby follow the path to freedom and healing. The goal, serenity, is within their grasp.

This is a new approach addressed to anyone who lives with the pain of a broken heart and who feels there is no hope, to anyone who is searching for a better life, a life filled with love and peace. In the hearts of all those whose stories we share throughout this work there has been a place for amazement, a place for a breakthrough, because these people have acknowledged their grief and their powerlessness.

In the time of Christ's birth, the old order had to do with enslavement, guilt, judgment, darkness and hostility, and no one could see how that could ever change. In our work, we meet many who have been rendered powerless, become enslaved by old categories and theories that tend to label them as problem people. Categories and theories are unfeeling terms that may place the possibility of healing beyond the reach of the ordinary person, and even at times beyond the power of the energizing, healing spirit of God. I do not attempt to explain each aspect of the breakthrough in these stories in traditional psychological terminology, because that would force the new energy into the old categories. The gospel reminds us that you cannot put new wine into old wineskins. (Matthew 9:17)

A newness is evident for us at Bountyfull: the healing of the broken-hearted has begun. Christ was born among the poor of society some 2000 years ago. Bountyfull, too, was born among the poor, the broken-hearted, those who have suffered as a result of the power-driven, money-hungry standards of our overindulgent consumer society.

We hope to continue to awaken that amazement in the broken-hearted in our world in this new millennium. Luke, in his gospel, summarized the whole movement of the birth of Christ in staggering simplicity:

> The blind receive their sight,
> the lame walk,
> lepers are cleansed,
> and the deaf hear,
> the dead are raised,
> the poor have the good news brought to them.
>
> *(Luke 7:22)*

Many of the people found on our streets in the east side of downtown Vancouver and Chinatown, where Bountyfull is located, fall into the above categories.

They are the blind; they see no hope, no future.

They are the lame; they stumble and fall on the pavement, curl up and seek shelter from the cold for the night and the new leprosy of AIDS is a rampant epidemic.

They are the deaf; they have closed their ears to all the criticism and advice and condemnation from society.

They hunger for a freedom from this death in which they are entombed.

To these, the poor, and any other person whose heart is broken and whose spirit is deadened by impossible burdens, to the thousands of people who have shared with us the joy of their breakthroughs over the past 17 years, I humbly address this work. In the words of Ezekiel,

> I will sprinkle clean water upon you, and you shall be clean from all your uncleannesses, and from all your idols I will cleanse you.... I will remove from your body the heart of stone and give you a heart of flesh...and you shall be my people, and I will be your God. (*Ezekiel 36:25-28*)

Invited to share our message are all those who sense that it is time for a breakthrough, an amazement, a new energy and a hope that the gospel promises, which sometimes seem to have been broken, are still being kept.

As part of our life's journey, we are all asked to discover the spiritual depths within ourselves, our own true "land," and to recapture the feeling that we, like Adam, are creatures of the earth. We are challenged to accept the divine invitation to be truly ourselves, children of earth, from dust to the divine. The divine energy, the Holy Spirit, yearns to emerge from the earthiness of our being, to enkindle the spark of the divine life that is deep within us, and finally, at the end of all our wanderings, to accept our true selves.

For us at Bountyfull, it is paramount that we keep in touch with the mystery of that divine energy, the Holy Spirit, moving within our being. This can be sensed only when we see our lives as stories, as an accumulation of happenings and experiences that are interwoven and given meaning when they are comprehended as stories. Our lives are not a succession of unrelated incidents; rather, they are a mysterious blending of the vast gamut of our experiences that make us unique. We have used the stories of people who have come to us with their permission, but have changed the names and some of the details to preserve their anonymity.

Throughout this book we shall glimpse the intimate sanctuary within the broken hearts of people who cry out for healing and strive to see meaning in the mystery of pain. I invite you to grant these stories the same sacredness with which every one of our staff members has honoured them throughout the years.

In sharing with you the wondrous journeys of those with whom we have walked, I hope that you will find the courage, strength and hope to embark on your own journey towards the fullness of life and find the serenity that awaits you.

We all share in the promise of that proclamation of Christ: "I came that they may have life, and have it abundantly" (John 10:10).

Larry Mackey, OMI
May 2004

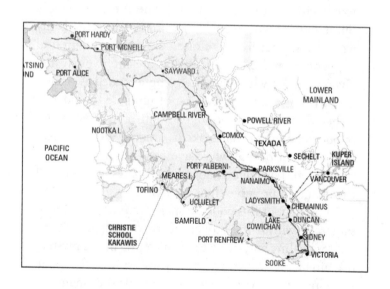

1

A Bountyfull History

Over 40 years ago, Christ's invitation to "Come, follow me" called me to my vocation as a missionary priest in the order of the Oblates of Mary Immaculate, whose motto is "The spirit of the Lord GOD is upon me, because the LORD has anointed me; he has sent me to bring the good news to the oppressed, to bind up the brokenhearted, to proclaim liberty to the captives" (Isaiah 61:1).

As a young priest I was studying to become a professor of St. Patrick's College, University of Ottawa. Every summer, at the end of the school year, all the students happily took off to go to the Oblates' summer camp, on Wapoos Island in Lake Ontario. Most of us were city boys and knew very little about farm life, but it was a welcome break from the books. Our main crop was peas; we had endless fields of them. When they were harvested it was my job to take them by scow to the mainland, a job I enjoyed, as I much preferred the water to the dusty fields. One day the boat stalled as I was towing the scow, and I was pinned between the scow and the wharf. That accident dislocated a few discs in my lower spine, and my long journey of pain and surgery began.

My superiors realized that I would be incapable of working as a university professor due to my inability to stand for any length of time. When I was released from hospital and back on my feet once again, I was assigned to the Indian missions on the west coast of British Columbia. I was very excited about beginning this new ministry, which fulfilled a lifelong dream. Once more I was filled with hope and a sense of challenge and adventure. In 1957 I was assigned to Kuper Island School, which served as the base for the surrounding missions in the Gulf Islands. It was to be my headquarters for the next few years, as I travelled to the outlying isolated missions, which could be reached only by boat. At first I used a small, open 16-foot outboard; later, I graduated to a 32-foot fishing boat that had no sleeping accommodations or galley. My job was to provide pastoral care for the Native people who lived in the area. Although their way of life and culture were totally foreign to me, I was asked to be present to them and help guide them on their spiritual journey. I had a lot to learn!

Over the seven years or so that I served these missions, I made many good friends among the people. I loved the simplicity of their way of life and their artistic expression, both in their carving and in their songs. I can still hear the resonant beat of the drums as they danced in the Big House. That beat of the drums and the dance on the earthen floor made me feel that the people were very close to the earth and to their creator. The drums were like the heartbeat of the people connecting them to their ancestors.

Together we built and repaired churches. Regularly, we celebrated Sunday Mass in the Kuper and Shell Beach Reserve churches. In the winter I would open up the church and split wood and start the fires to heat the building. I established a catechetical course for young children, and marriage and baptismal preparation for adults.

On the lighter side, I helped set up a homemakers' club for the women on the Shell Beach Reserve, and purchased half a dozen sewing machines, which they put to good use for their families. In the basement of the church there, we occasionally hosted square dances. For the men, I supported the soccer teams and, above all, the canoe-pulling teams. Canoe-pulling is a sport that is surrounded with festivity and much competition. I recall a memorable journey to compete in the canoe races in North Vancouver. I strapped a 12-man canoe to the top of my boat, the *Stella Maris*, and took off in the late evening from Kuper Island with 10 Native people aboard, including a mother and a nursing baby, to go to Vancouver – 40 miles across the open sea. The seas were very heavy and, to add to the challenge, we began to take on water. I was afraid the bilge water would splash on the open spark plugs and cause the motor to stall. My bilge pump was missing, and so we mustered all the hands on board to fill the pots and pans the ladies had brought for cooking and bail the water overboard. It took us about four hours to stem the flow of water during this five-hour journey. I was so happy to see the lights of Vancouver in the early morning!

Then a new scourge hit all the reserves in British Columbia, including those under my care. In the mid-

1950s, the government finally allowed the Native people to buy liquor and take it home to their reserves. Before long, the easy access to liquor began to devastate their peaceful and deeply spiritual lifestyle. In order to help counteract the evils wrought by liquor, I helped establish the first program of Alcoholics Anonymous (AA) on Kuper Island in about 1959.

The Central Office of AA in Victoria sent a representative to Kuper Island to help set up the program. Many people responded very well to the program because they were greatly concerned about the ravages of alcohol among their families and children. I fondly remember the meetings at Kuper Island because of the phenomenal sense of humour of the Native people as they related what were often tragic stories with a unique storytelling flair, often making fun of themselves. Their openness and honesty was refreshing, and they rarely missed the weekly meetings.

From Kuper Reserve, AA programs spread to Cowichan through Fr. Rossiter, an Oblate friend of mine, and a friendly rivalry began between the two groups. Living on the island, I found it a foreboding challenge to return from an AA meeting in Cowichan in the dark across five miles of open sea on the *Stella Maris*, watching for the many logs that floated on the water. Yet the hardships only increased my determination to keep the groups going. On a recent visit to Kuper Island I was happy to see that the group is still meeting, and some of the old members are still sober and successfully employed.

In 1964 I became the administrator of Christie School at Kakawis on Meares Island, just off Tofino on the beautiful west coast of Vancouver Island. Even though I was the administrator of the residence, I maintained my enthusiasm for the AA program. I brought a few of the members from the Kuper Island group with me, and we started an AA program at Opitsat Reserve in 1964. From those humble beginnings, the AA program continued to spread along the west coast of the island.

My love of the sea would turn out to be my downfall. Eventually, the relentless battering of the ocean waves took its toll on my spine, and I found myself back in hospital for a series of spinal surgeries. By the early 1980s, I was in a wheelchair, with very little hope that I would fully recover. I realized that my missionary dreams of life on the open sea, on the rugged west coast of Vancouver Island, were a thing of the past.

My superiors decided that, due to my physical disability, I could no longer stand and preach at church, and transferred me to our provincial house in Vancouver. There I was assigned full-time to the ministry of "5th-step work," part of AA's 12-step program. The 4th step of AA asks members to "make a searching and fearless moral inventory" of their whole lives. Following that, people are guided in Step 5 to "admit to God, ourselves and another human being, the exact nature of our wrongs."

Through the program, men and women are challenged to become aware of and to openly admit their powerlessness over alcohol, and to turn their lives over to the God of their understanding. This idea of admitting one's powerlessness put me in touch with my own recent journey with my disability, and with the rhythm of the Old Testament prophets, whom I had loved for many years. Jeremiah, the prophet before the exile, grieved for the land that his people had loved and lost. Isaiah, on the other hand, was the prophet of hope. He foretold the coming of the Christ and freedom from sin. These prophets taught me that we can never realize the fullness of hope in a newness of life until we have faced our powerlessness and grieved the loss of our dreams.

Today it is difficult for many people to grieve. Our affluent lifestyles have caused us to become satiated, and we are distracted by the tools of modern technology. The broken people of our world often dull their senses by self-medicating and sedating their pain. Healing can come only when people admit to their powerlessness and grieve the loss of their peace and serenity.

I discovered that the mysterious spiritual power of this simple program could put people in touch with their powerlessness and open their hearts to the healing hand of God. I saw that the concept of prisoners, found in the text quoted from Isaiah, was a much broader term than I had traditionally understood. My life as a missionary among people who faced intolerable difficulties and pain broadened my vision. It was more than the prisons of stone, steel bars and guards, which spoke of confinement and loss of freedom: "prisoners" included many people who freely walk the streets and yet live within the prisons of their own making. Their prisons are forged by fear, guilt, rejection and pain, and hold them captive within their own beings.

In this 5th-step ministry, I met many people who were bearing heavy burdens of pain, fear and guilt. These were the broken-hearted, the wounded, living within the dark dungeons of their buried pain, perhaps since early childhood. I felt called to this in-depth healing process with people who would come to me, one at a time. I came to understand that my clients alone held the key to release their deeply buried pain, because only they could access their own personal experiences. Even as adults they were still prisoners of their past. They had to be helped to find the courage and faith to enter into those fearful memories, to dispel the demons of the past and to bravely choose to be set free, to reach out a pleading hand towards God's healing forgiveness, to choose what was meaningful and life-giving for them.

I had walked a painful journey in my own physical disabilities. Now, despite my disability, my priestly calling would have meaning once more. In a very real way, I felt that I had a common bond with the pain of broken-hearted and wounded people.

2

The Process Develops

Christ's promise of abundant life is over 2000 years old. Sadly, our world still seems so torn apart, and many people still live with pain, loneliness and brokenness.

When we bought Bountyfull House as the base for our work on inner healing, it seemed appropriate that our healing centre should be located in an area with such an obvious need for some solution, however modest, to the devastation caused by drugs, alcohol, depression and mental breakdown.

Today, the most visible forms of brokenness in our clients are addictions to alcohol, drugs, food and sex. It is so easy to label people with these destructive behavioural patterns as dysfunctional. It is so easy to look at the alcoholic or drug addict and feel, with a certain sense of self-satisfaction and righteousness, that *they* have the problem. We can categorize them and study them because *their* problems are so obvious. Of course, all of us have need of healing at some level, even though we might not recognize it or admit it.

Very early on, this work sensitized me to the crying need people have for some type of deep inner healing. I felt called to respond to that need. This was a very different field of missionary activity – the vast, uncharted area of repressed pain and anguish within the human heart. My missionary calling was no longer simply a matter of pushing back geographical frontiers, but rather of exploring new frontiers of deep spiritual healing within the human soul.

For us at Bountyfull, the spiritual aspect is central: our hope is to help people raise their vision beyond simply coping with problems to developing a sense of energy and craving for a fuller, meaningful life, a life in union with God.

Abundant Life

Christ's promise, "I came that they may have life, and have it abundantly," resonated throughout my whole being and filled me with hope, energy, and a yearning for a greater understanding of the mystery of life. Very early it awakened in me a hunger to know what this promise could mean for me in my own life, and in the lives of others. I wanted to discover how to unlock the dynamism and hidden source of energy in that simple word "life."

In my search I meditated often on the gospel images that Christ used: the tiny seed that held the promise of a huge mustard tree, or the mystery of the mighty oak. I imagined the life cycle of the seed that had to fall into the ground and die before it could break through into new life. The gospel of John states, "Unless the seed falls into the ground and dies it remains alone, but if it dies it bears much fruit" (John 12:24). I was fascinated by the idea that the shell that protected the great treasure of new life had to be broken through, or broken open, before the mystery of growth could take place.

The Mystery of Self-movement

Before we begin to probe the spiritual and psychological problems that we face as human beings, I would like to share what I see as a simple understanding of the dynamism of our life's energy. I pondered the psychological insights of Thomas Aquinas, in which he defines the ineffable gift of life as "the power to move oneself from within," or, more simply, the power of self-movement. The intellectual definition had great clarity, but it lacked the dynamism and energy of what I had experienced in observing living, moving beings. To me, the definition was the bare bones of the great mystery of life that is God's gift to each of us. I have found great joy and freedom in moving beyond the constraints of the confining concepts of definitions. I have always thrilled to the realization that one of our greatest gifts – and one that is sometimes given very poor press – is the gift of our imaginations, which allows us to use our creativity to develop the talents God has given us.

The concept of movement intrigued me. I always knew that we can be moved physically by some external force, either positively or negatively, but I never realized that, even more wondrously, we possess the power to move ourselves from within. I was fascinated to discover what stimulates or activates our life power and causes us to move, or be moved, from within – intellectually, psychologically or spiritually.

Prayerfully, I probed the insights that would open up the mystery of that hidden power of self-movement, which, by its very nature, is open to the life-giving spirit of God.

Youthful Awe and Wonder

I was born in Iroquois Falls, Ontario, and grew up in the north. Early in my childhood, I was enthralled with the beauty of nature. I was in awe in winter as the gently falling, delicate snowflakes wrapped the whole world in a silent white blanket. Lakes, mountains, rocks, trees became transformed by this shroud of white. Before too long, spring was on its way; I marvelled at how our sleeping world threw off that blanket and, suddenly and miraculously, myriad forms of new life burst into being with a mesmerizing array of sounds, colours and smells.

Years later, I found my impressions echoed in the childlike wisdom of Francis Thompson in his poem "Shelley" (the last four lines are quoting William Blake):

Know you what it is to be a child? It is to be something very different from the man of today. It is to have a spirit yet streaming from the waters of baptism; it is to believe in love, to believe in loveliness, to believe in belief; it is to be so little that the elves can reach to whisper in your ear; it is to turn pumpkins into coaches, and mice into horses, lowness into loftiness, and nothing into everything, for each child has its fairy godmother in its own soul; it is to live in a nutshell and to count yourself the king of infinite space; it is

To see a world in a grain of sand,
And a Heaven in a wild flower,
Hold infinity in the palm of your hand,
And eternity in an hour....

I was captivated not only by this sense of wonder, but by the thought that we as human beings are "fearfully and wonderfully made" (Psalm 139:14). Where does this elusive fountain of youthful energy and wonder come from? Is it something that youths alone possess, or can we be aware at every stage of that depth, that wisdom, that life-power and energy within us? We are challenged to look within the depths of our own being, to find the resonant notes of the deeply inspiring word of God. God is saying that we are fragile vessels of clay that are the receptacles of his life-giving spirit.

How is the beauty of the external world transformed into the energy and dynamism of life-power? How does this mystery come to pass? Above all, how do we make this mystery of life comprehensible, something that we can consciously work with in order to develop our capacity to be more fully alive?

I have often watched in wonder when a little child spurns the gift of an expensive technological toy and chooses to sit in fascination with the shining brilliance and the clanging noise of something as simple as a spoon. That childlike freedom and joy at the wonder of life spurred my imagination to create a simple way to comprehend for myself the great psychological mystery of the human person.

The Gift of Our Imagination

To preserve that sense of simplicity and wonder, I replaced the child's shining, clanging spoon with a playful diagram that captures the mystery of the dynamism in the power of self-movement in a very simple way. This diagram began to unlock for me the treasure of the source of that elusive life spirit that is our source of energy. I drew a little "toy man" and invested him with all the gifts of wisdom that psychology and philosophy had taught me. Doing this allowed me to live in my imagination and watch in fascination as the child reaches out to the wonder-filled reality of creation, bringing the wealth of the external world into the sanctuary of the inner self. As I played with this little toy man that I had devised, I could feel the flow of energy that allowed it to come to life. I spent hours solving deep psychological mysteries with the little toy man.

The Toy Man Diagram

Our spirits and receptive powers are open to the great wonder of creation, and our hearts crave fullness and unity with our creator. Thomas Aquinas defines human beings as "rational animals," possessing both a body and a soul. In faithfulness to this definition, I drew the little toy man with both a body and a soul. I depicted the body's functions on the left side, and the soul and its spiritual functions on the right side. I drew a horizontal line across the diagram: the top half depicted our receptive powers, both sensory and intellectual; the bottom half, our affective powers. Our affective powers are both our spiritual powers to choose, which we call willpower, and our bodily appetites that motivate us to seek the objects of our choice.

In the following diagram I have drawn four quadrants in order to help distinguish the different functions of both our bodily senses and our intellectual or spiritual gifts. I hasten to point out that there is no line of demarcation or division between the body and the soul, or between our receptive powers and our affective abilities. These are merely distinctions I have made in order to grasp something of the wonder of a living being.

TOY MAN Life = *power of self-movement*

1 Toy Man – an insight into what moves us to act – gives us <u>Energy</u>

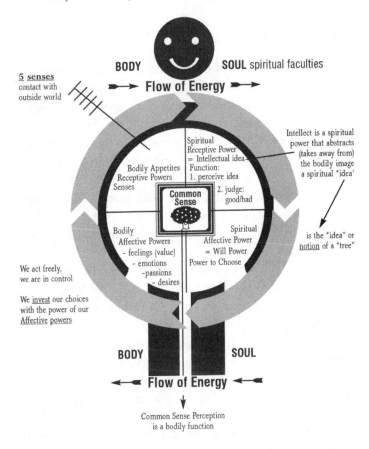

BODY

SOUL spiritual faculties

<u>5 senses</u>
contact with
outside world

Flow of Energy ➤➤

Spiritual
Receptive Power
= Intellectual idea
Function:
1. perceive idea

Intellect is a spiritual
power that abstracts
(takes away from)
the bodily image
a spiritual "idea"

Bodily Appetites
Receptive Powers
Senses

2. judge:
good/bad

Common Sense

is the "idea" or
<u>notion</u> of a "tree"

Bodily
Affective Powers
- feelings (value)
- emotions
-passions
- desires

Spiritual
Affective Power
= Will Power
Power to Choose

We act freely,
we are in control

We <u>invest</u> our choices
with the power of our
<u>Affective</u> <u>powers</u>

BODY

SOUL

◄◄ **Flow of Energy** ◄

Common Sense Perception
is a bodily function

29

My imaginative description of the little toy man helped me understand the more complicated psychological functions.

Toy Man: First Quadrant

To contemplate the awakening of that life energy within the spirit of a child, I depicted the child's ability to contact the unbelievable reality of the beauty of God's creation in the external world. I did this by placing a little TV aerial in the first quadrant. On this little aerial I placed five channels to represent our five senses. I marvelled at how the slow awakening of the five senses – taste, touch, hearing, sight and smell – carry the indescribable sensations of the wonder of creation to the child's world, and at the wealth this brings to his or her human experience.

In order to capture the richness of the information that these "channels" deliver, I drew a little TV monitor within the centre of the toy man's being, and there imagined all the symbols of his experience on the screen. We collate all the findings of our external senses in a function that has been called the "common sense." In the toy man, I show how his imagination began to create exciting symbols of the physical world of his experience on this little TV screen which, for me, was a symbol of the common sense. Children do not develop intellectual ability until they approach what we call the age of reason at approximately seven years of age. Until then, they live in symbol and in sense perception.

This insight allowed me to understand how the child can be so enthralled with the simple sense perception of a spoon, for example.

Toy Man: Second Quadrant

In the second quadrant of the little toy man, I indicated our intellectual ability to abstract or form a concept or idea from what the senses had perceived. The intellect operates as a spiritual power that can abstract, or take away, from the sense symbol a meaningful idea that is an intellectual comprehension of the physical object. The intellect has a twofold function of perceiving and judging what is beneath the microscope of our mind.

I drew a little light bulb in the second quadrant to signify the development of an idea, spiritual notion or concept that is formed in our ego, or our conscious awareness. The ego is our organizational centre; it retains the complex of our psychic facts that we have perceived from the external world, whether it be that of a tree, an apple, or a person, for example. Our ego organizes our relationships with the outside world into fixed patterns or constellations which, in Jungian terminology, are called complexes. In order to grasp the meaningfulness of how we constellate the information our external senses perceive, I depicted a magnet drawing metal filings to itself. In this same way, we become trained to draw external reality into the channels of our senses and firmly constellate them or form them into fixed, receptive channels. For example, each culture is stamped with these "learned" and "fixed" behavioural patterns in which the child grows up and becomes a committed member of that particular culture. As we see in the turmoil of our world, tradition and religious observance have become fixed constellations of our ability to interpret and organize the spiritual reality that guides our lives. In very graphic ways, we see how individuals and nations will fight to the death to preserve the heritage of their culture. The Acts of the Apostles gives us a graphic example of how the Israelites in the time of Jesus fought defiantly against this change: "...for we have heard him say that this Jesus of Nazareth will destroy this place and will change the customs that Moses handed on to us" (Acts 6:14).

We develop many other less basic forms of constellations that become learned behavioural patterns. We are reluctant to change them, however necessary that change may be. These constellations and complexes become almost autonomous, as if they have their own personality. For example, children who are victimized when they are young can form what we call a "victim complex." They will live their whole lives in a victim role out of fear because when they were young they were trained to feel like a victim. Another common complex is the inferiority complex, which children can easily develop if they feel they are less worthy than one of their siblings in the eyes of their parents or significant others. They build around themselves a shell of a sense of inferiority and find it very difficult to break through that perception and acknowledge their own self-worth.

I thrilled to the realization that children could begin to name all the wonders of creation and could file them all away in their memory without taking up any space, because these notions or concepts are spiritual realities.

In that manner children begin to create their own treasure chest, retaining what has made the greatest impact on their lives, whether it be a life-giving and meaningful memory of being loved and cared for or, alternatively, the dark and painful memories of the past.

Toy Man: Third Quadrant

In the third quadrant I depicted our spiritual power to choose what we have judged as good for us or to reject what is harmful. We develop what we have termed our willpower to the degree that we invest our ability to choose with energy and commitment and strength.

We may think of the will as the power that comes with force and determination, but in reality it is the God-given gift of our ability to choose, to will what we perceive as good for us and to reject what is evil and takes our life spirit away. We may have seen the will as a driving power that motivates our actions with a firm hand, but in reality, it is our power to choose what is life-giving. When we value something as being meaningful and fulfilling, then that power to choose well becomes very strong. When we turn our energy and our will to choose something with great meaning and purpose, our lives can become much richer, and we rise above the negativity that has taken our strength away.

Toy Man: Fourth Quadrant

As we look at the little toy man, we can almost feel the surge of energy move from the bottom right quadrant of the willpower, where we have determined the object of our choice, to the fourth quadrant, in the bottom left corner, where we invest this choice with the power of the bodily affects. The intellectual choice of something good is then invested with all the richness and beauty and desirability of our bodily appetites, which encompass all our meaningful desires and emotions and add so much personal quality and value to our lives.

The God-given gifts of our affective bodily powers bring a life-giving surge to our being and allow us to feel the energy flowing within us to give the dynamism and the motivation we need to achieve our goals. Energy flows through us and we move ourselves freely from within. In a word, we are motivated. This is our life-power or the power of self-movement.

Conversely, when children experience the bodily pain of being beaten or violently punished, or the spiritual pain of rejection, the negativity leaves an indelible scar on their soul. They shut down the appetitive functions, retire within, and build a protective shell around themselves. The wonder of a child's world can be shattered on the rocks of disappointment and rejection in very little time.

As I allowed my imagination to develop this little toy man, I felt that I had not only understood something of the meaning of the psychological terms, but that I could watch a person move or grow or come into fullness of life. I acquired a greater comprehension of how a person becomes stimulated or moved, either by an external force, or even more powerfully, by a spiritual force from within; this clarified for me the dynamic in the spiritual concept of "inspiration." I could almost sense how God breathes into us his life-giving power and love.

That simple toy man I drew allowed me to understand better how life works. It helped me to grasp many of the sophisticated notions of the science of psychology, and it has been the underlying source of the wisdom that has guided me over the years in healing ministry at Bountyfull. It helped me to become involved in my own journey of psychological healing and spiritual growth, to see how the direct inspiration of the Holy Spirit can be brought into the sanctuary of our psyche and move us from within. People who are deeply contemplative and close to the love of God do not need explanations and reasoning to deepen their faith; their hearts are open to receive. Like children, they respond immediately to the message of love; they are filled with that life-giving energy of the spirit of God.

Energized by the "Voice of God"

The Bountyfull insight of probing the mysterious depths of broken hearts was born from the pain of my own brokenness. Every day since I began to do this work, I have been privileged to relive something of that same mystery with almost every person who has come through our doors at Bountyfull. For years I've been able to cope with chronic back pain and sleepless nights by moving beyond my own pain and resonating with the healing, life-giving message from the heart of someone who is broken and yearning to be whole.

My focus has always been the wonder that a person can live through agony and pain, and yet come to a fuller life. I became attuned to the voice of God in the cry of the broken, rather than becoming overwhelmed or inundated by the countless revelations of people's unbearable pain, agony and depression. I have been energized by the thrill of sensing that deeply hidden, yet ever-present, voice of God crying out for someone to listen and to respond with a healing heart. I have learned to read beneath the recitation of horrendous brokenness to help people find their spirit surging within themselves and yearning to be free.

With this insight, I did not have to teach myself not to take on people's pain, or their endless fight for freedom, or their struggle to overcome injustice. I live with the firm conviction that when people get in touch with their true selves and set themselves free, with the power of God they take back their own lives and successfully deal with whatever problems arise. During a session this allows me to move beyond theorizing and categorizing, and enables me to touch the heart of someone who is a total stranger, yearning for that promise of life to the full.

One day I sat at the bedside of a dear friend who was dying. With her whole family she had suffered terribly during their imprisonment in Japan during World War II. Their family had been separated. Her husband was sent to one concentration camp; she and their children had to survive without him in another camp. Yet she never lost her spirit. Her faith and hope gave her the energy to carry on. In the last few moments of her life she said, "Father Larry, I want to leave this thought with you: 'energy' is a deeply spiritual term that is very meaningful for our world today."

Since that moment, I have become much more aware of the profound mystery of energy. It means much more than the fuels – nuclear, electric and fossil – that move our world, or the kinetic process that allows us to move. "Energy" is a much more dynamic word when we contemplate being filled with the never-ending, life-giving energy of the Spirit of God. In his parting words in the gospel of Matthew, Christ gives us this assurance: "And remember, I am with you always, to the end of the age (Matthew 28:20)."

Sense Memory

Over time I began to understand something of the marvel of the world of the senses and all of the delicate realities that are somehow stored in our intellect and filed in our memory. I became aware of the highly developed sense memory within the animal kingdom, as was demonstrated by Pavlov in his experiment with conditioned responses in dogs. Not only do animals have acute sensitive powers, they have unbelievable retention of their sense perception. They have an unquestioning response to their master and jealously protect their own turf and their master's possessions.

In one very moving incident, a client named "Cindy," whose story we will hear in Chapter 8, described how her sister's dog, Cocoa, was the one who let Cindy know that her sister was dead. Her sister lived alone in an isolated area outside the city limits, and Cocoa was her only companion. When she was murdered, Cocoa traced his way 10 miles across busy Vancouver streets and sat, dirty, wet and tired, on the doorstep of the home where it had lived as a pup. Cocoa's arrival prompted Cindy to search for her sister.

Endless examples of the miracle of sense perception and sense memory remind me that we, too, have acute sensory memories because we are part of the animal kingdom. How often have we experienced the difficulty of letting go or forgiving someone who has hurt us and taken our life spirit away? We know we must forgive, and yet that pain of the past is so deeply etched within our being that it is difficult to let it go. Christ reminds us that we must forgive not with our head alone, but from our heart (Matthew 18:21-35).

Our intellectual gifts and powers can move us from within, probing the filing cabinet that stores our memory of things past to relive what has touched us or given meaning in our lives. In this way, the little toy man has helped me to trace the trail of broken hearts of the clients who have come to us for healing.

The Dynamism of Words and Actions

I began to watch for dynamism in words and actions. What energizes people? What moves people? What is the hidden power in words or actions or symbols or simple thoughts that inspires people? I also started to notice relational components. What is the dynamism, the mystery, the power in personal relationships? How do people relate to each other? I found that there is a dynamic in this interpersonal relationship, an interaction, even without words, so that simply being in another person's presence can move us.

We have all observed how the whole ambience of a room can change when a certain person enters. If that person is filled with anger or passive aggression, the spirit of the room loses energy. If someone who is positive, energetic and free comes on the scene, the energy in the room immediately picks up and generates further peace and freedom. Children have become very important in the therapeutic process in geriatric wards or palliative care. It is heart-warming to observe how little children can defuse tense situations or heavy moods with their carefree enjoyment of life. An affectionate animal can also raise the spirits of sick and lonely people, because it offers an unconditional, trusting acceptance.

The functioning of this wondrous creature, the human person, can easily be disrupted. The energy source for self-movement can be blocked or deadened, and the spirit, the life force, crushed. This is what happens when someone chooses destructive behavioural patterns. We see this brokenness manifested in a variety of behaviours: addiction to alcohol or drugs, as well as compulsive eating, working, sex, gambling, shopping, watching TV, surfing the Internet…the list is endless.

Rising Above

Early in my life, I developed a yearning for serenity and peace and depth. Around age five, growing up in Noranda, I wished I could rise above the pain of loneliness and rejection in my own childlike way. My dad was a logger and was therefore seldom at home. He spent most of his time out in the woods. I can still see him taking off in a small plane into the vast hinterlands of northern Ontario. He would be gone for days, weeks or even months. I felt that he could simply take off and fly free, get above it all and see the big picture. I, on the other hand, was just a little kid. I had to stay on the ground and be confined to my dreary, though lovingly supported, existence at home with mom, my siblings and the daily routine. I can still recall longingly searching the skies for Dad's return. Often, I could see the plane as a distant speck that gradually grew until it came into full view. I would always know when it was Dad's plane because his friend Roy Brown, the celebrated World War I pilot, would buzz our house. That feeling of Dad's coming back home gave me a deep sense of excitement and filled me with energy and peace. It was always good to have him back.

I used to love looking at the faded brown photographs Dad took with his old box camera picturing his life in the woods, canoeing on distant rivers in the summer and snowshoeing in the winter. I still have a few of those old photographs where Dad ("Slim") stood tall in his snowshoes in the deep snow of a frozen lake surrounded by forests and hills. He told me how he learned to survive alone in that vast winterland, how he pitched his tent and built a little firepit in the snow at his feet to keep him warm, and made a bed of cedar boughs for his eiderdown sleeping bag. Later on in life, the "smelly sleeping bag" that bothered Mom so much transported me back in fantasy to the sacred silence of the frozen north. I remember a few lines of his poetry that spoke of his closeness to God and nature:

Come lie beneath the pines and rest
and ease your mind of earthly sorrow
for pines will tell you that man is blest
and he shall have tomorrow.

I loved how he lived so close to nature and the Native people, and remember the great respect he had for them. I recall especially the story of how two Native women came regularly by canoe to nurse him through a severe illness when he was stranded alone in the woods. These stories gave me a sense of peace and allowed me to transcend what was happening in my limited existence at home.

Dad experienced that love and joy of living in a very deep and peaceful way. I, too, became captivated by the mystery of life. That love of life and the sense of being free has stayed with me all these years and has kept my spirit alive, through good times and hard times.

The Mystery of Story

In my childlike fantasy I took off on wings to experience thrilling adventures and challenges far beyond the narrow confines of my own humble home. I experienced the mystery of how stories offer a way of seeing in the dark. This became a great gift to me later on in my work as I realized that, when people confront the darkness in their journeys, telling this as a story that encompasses both weakness and strength eases the difficulty. Such personalization and ownership bring about a sense of possession and confidence. Almost unconsciously, as they view their lives as unique stories, people raise their vision to rise above the present problem and grasp the total picture, rather than remaining mired in the burden of their pain and powerlessness.

Our story can be a great gift because it not only brings relief and peace as it unfolds, but it also engenders a mysterious sense of joy, as if it were a vicarious experience of someone else's journey. It sets us free from anxiety, fear and guilt, and allows us to see new visions, new hopes on distant horizons.

This symbol of rising above it all became an important part of my teaching skills as I incorporated it in the charting and healing procedures we use in sessions at Bountyfull.

Our healing insight is based on the Serenity Prayer: "God, grant me the serenity to accept the things I cannot change, the courage to change the things I can, and the wisdom to know the difference." This prayer guides us to accept our whole life story as it is, and to call on the power of God to give us the strength to let go of our painful past. The symbol of coming back home became an inspiration for the healing process at Bountyfull House. We conclude all our healing sessions and group meetings by adding to the Serenity Prayer our own unique signature with this simple phrase: "Keep coming home – it works." Home to our real self, home to our hearts in which we feel grounded and whole within our being.

We Are Middle People

People do not find it easy to tell their stories chronologically. Author and storyteller John Shea has said that we are "middle people"; we are usually so overwhelmed with our present problems and related feelings that we can't see the total life picture. To help people to comprehend and to visualize their stories and to reconnect with the meaningful memories of their past,

I devised the idea of using a 3- x 5-foot flip chart to record the various incidents they relate as their stories unfold. The visualization, the graphic images and the subtle lines that I draw between various events or relationships helps to make visible and comprehensible these numinous, intangible realities.

I use charts and stick figures to encompass the whole picture, to help people see their present problems in perspective, to rise above them and to embrace their whole life story. This visual representation of their story allows them to look beyond the heavy burdens that have imprisoned their spirits. Slowly, their spirits are awakened; they rise above the pain and embarrassment of their guilt and shame as they follow the pathway back to their early childhood.

When we trace the timeline from a present trauma back to early childhood and they watch their story unfold, people discover a whole new awareness and a sense of freedom. So often during these sessions, I have seen their joy and relief when they exclaim, "I can see it all now, right there in front of me. Now I understand!"

In our ministry at Bountyfull House, I have a sense of the welcoming and healing ministry of Christ at the Last Supper, when he knelt before the disciples and washed their feet. To me, their feet symbolize the pathways they have walked in their lives. When Christ washed their feet, he absolved and washed away the pain of their past.

The concept of the little toy man and the symbols of "rising above it all" and "coming back home" allowed me to see each life as a story, and to glimpse something of that great mystery of Christ's promise that he has come that we "may have life, and have it abundantly."

Bountyfull Vision: From Darkness to Light

This is the vision of healing that inspires and energizes us at Bountyfull. Our focus is the uniqueness of the person and the mystery of life within. With childlike simplicity, which is understandable to professional and layperson alike, we look at the profound mystery of the human person and the power of life that surges within us from the earliest moments of conception. We aim for a better understanding of how we interact and relate with this wondrous creation to which we belong – nature, family, society and the mystery of God.

3

Pilgrims from Foreign Lands

I will take you from the nations, and gather you from all
the countries, and bring you into your own land. I will
sprinkle clean water upon you, and you shall be clean from
all your uncleannesses; from all your idols I will cleanse you.
    A new heart I will give you, and a new spirit I will
put within you; and I will remove from your body the
heart of stone and give you a heart of flesh. I will put my
spirit within you, and make you follow my statutes and be
careful to observe my ordinances. Then you shall live in
the land that I gave to your ancestors; and you shall be my
people, and I will be your God.

(Ezekiel 36:24-28)

This text from the prophet Ezekiel poignantly paints
a picture of the Israelites who had been exiled and
wandering for many years in foreign countries, yearning
to return to the land of their ancestors. God hears their
cries and promises to bring them home to their own land
and to give them a newness of heart. Many parables and
familiar phrases that we freely quote from scripture hold
a profound healing message. The living word of God
applies not only to the plight of the Israelites, but probes
right to the root of the problem within our broken hearts.

In this text from Ezekiel, the key is to be aware of the broader meaning of "foreign lands."

These words could apply to many people who leave the "homeland" of their real selves and unconsciously live in foreign lands within themselves, deserts in which they merely survive. The desert does not nourish them or slake their thirst, but ultimately leads to their loss of spirit and loss of life. Many of these wanderers slip into a morass of depression, are overwhelmed by self-pity, erupt with self-righteous anger and violence, and can be completely taken out of themselves in uncontrollable rage and passion.

Each morning as I drive to work through what is often described as "the war zone," I observe people huddling in the cold and the rain, seeking cover in doorways or bus shelters where they have spent the night. Down the lanes and back alleys, others blatantly traffic in drugs or shoot up. All of this happens literally within the shadow of the police station at Main and Hastings. Within the downtown core of Vancouver, people are exiled to the foreign lands of despair and dejection. At Bountyfull, we are only too conscious that "like a roaring lion, your adversary the devil prowls around, looking for someone to devour" (1 Peter 5:8).

Peter's Challenge

In this day and age, we hesitate to speak about Satan, the power of the devil, the presence of an evil spirit that seeks to destroy. The concept of Satan or the devil is considered not only medieval, but archaic and meaningless in a world that is wrapped securely in technological expertise and control. The power of evil is so subtle that it cannot easily be discerned and dealt with. We can only become aware of its presence by observing its devastating effects as it wreaks havoc in human lives.

In June 1999, that realization was deeply affirmed for me as I listened to news coverage of the International AIDS Symposium in Vancouver. This gathering involved professionals from all over the world addressing the crisis of HIV/AIDS epidemic and related problems in Vancouver's downtown east side. At the end of the program, after all the theories on possible solutions had been presented, Peter, a recovering addict, observed that from his experience, drugs, alcohol and other chemical substances are primarily means to numb pain. People self-medicate pain to cope with their hopelessness and powerlessness. Peter, who yearned to be free of his addiction, asked a pointed question: "Who is addressing that pain and how can it be relieved?" The panel's response was that although this is a pertinent question, society does not have an adequate solution.

Peter's challenge to the social service providers of the world seemed overwhelming in the face of the mountains of evidence presented at this symposium. The broken people, the pilgrims we see on our city streets, understandably draw the attention of concerned and caring people. They obviously pose a phenomenal problem for the social services of the city. This vision of such a massive problem seemed to leave the experts and others feeling powerless.

Peter's frustration and pain, and the symposium panel's response, resonated in me. I was reminded of

Christ's words when he approached the tomb of Lazarus: "He cried with a loud voice, 'Lazarus, come out!' The dead man came out, his hands and feet bound with strips of cloth, and his face wrapped in a cloth. Jesus said to them, 'Unbind him, and let him go.'" (John 11:43-44)

When we read this gospel text, we may focus on the historical event and marvel at the miracle Jesus performed. But this story speaks to all of us who are bound or imprisoned in some way. Christ is challenging the many broken people in our society who are powerless and trapped within their painful addictions, but he invites all of us – whatever our life stories may be – to move from death to new life.

All of us, all hurting people, like Lazarus, are called to come out of the tombs of our imprisonment. Our tombs may have been built with the brick, mortar and steel of our repressed anger, our buried hatred and the resentments that protect our broken hearts. We may lie dead within the tombs of our imprisoned spirits. Christ will roll back the stone of these tombs, but we, the community, must work together to unbind the cloths that have bound us. Thread by thread, we unbind our imprisoned spirits to set ourselves, and others, free.

I have deeply felt the anguish and pain of people whose spirits have become constrained or imprisoned by addiction rooted in denied or buried feelings. Like the giant in Jonathan Swift's allegorical book *Gulliver's Travels*, who is secured to the ground by the little people of Lilliput with thousands of thin gossamer threads while he sleeps, the men and women who come to me for help are bound by those imperceptible, painful threads from their past and have become totally powerless.

I sense that their hearts have become bound by the imperceptible web of buried feelings, shattered hopes and broken dreams. Their life spirit is rendered totally powerless by the depressing darkness of that cloud of denied feelings.

The giant's liberation comes only when these little gossamer threads are cut, one by one. Our work at Bountyfull is not unlike the work of the little people of Lilliput. We are sensitive to these thin, gossamer-like threads that bind hearts and imprison people by taking their spirit away.

How do we find a meaningful solution to people's problems and, at the same time, embrace a vision that will energize all broken-hearted people to rise above their plight? In facing our problems we are encouraged by Christ's words of encouragement: "The one who believes in me will also do the works that I do and, in fact, will do greater works than these" (John 14:12).

The Bountyfull program is a breakthrough in accessing that pain buried within the hearts of broken people. For years we have worked with many people from self-help groups (AA, Al-Anon, Narcotics Anonymous, etc.) who strive to face their powerlessness and their inability to live a meaningful life. When I earnestly respond to the cry of the poor and the broken-hearted, which to me is the voice of God, I see many signs that people we work with are unbound and set free. Our goal is to help people uncover the deeply buried roots of their pain by retracing the pathways of their life stories. It is our experience, and our firm conviction, that such pain can be accessed and people can be set free. That is the hope and the mission to which we commit ourselves at Bountyfull House.

As we progress with this insight, I invite you to reflect on your own life story while I share the stories of people who have openly and honestly revealed their own pain and brokenness. Because we all tend to develop ways of acting or coping in order to escape pain or to protect our broken hearts, we can all learn from each other's experiences.

Exiled in Foreign Lands

Many of the unfortunate people on our city streets are truly foreigners from distant countries, but all are living as pilgrims in the frightening lands within themselves, lands to which any one of us can flee in fear and pain. These dark places, the chambers in our memories, harbour our silent anger and hatred, our guilt and loneliness, our frustration, brokenness and despair. We yearn to be freed from these demons. We crave a new heart and a new spirit, and long to return to the homeland of our true selves.

Dynamic Feeling-toned Phraseology

The language of violence and anger, which I call "dynamic feeling-toned phraseology," conceals hidden pain. This language of slavery is unique to each one of us; it is rooted in our personal story, picked up unconsciously from the land of our birth, our family of origin, our early childhood, when we experienced the original pain. It is the language and behaviour of coping and survival. Perhaps it was our response to the spoken language of those who were in charge of us, who ignored us or, alternatively, smothered us with attention. It may have been our response to a puzzling, silent language whose underlying message instilled fear and dread. It may have been our response to violent, terrifying outbursts and beatings that caused us to recoil in pain and become almost paralyzed.

It is not a language of freedom: it is the language of reaction, fear and defence. In the midst of confusion and pain, a child develops his or her own coping skills and language. These coping skills or survival techniques are a joy to rediscover as we walk back along the path of our stories. Some of us may have been taught that our childhood behaviour was deviant, disobedient or sinful. Yet at the time, it was our means of survival, and often a clever one at that. It was a language of deception. We baffled the adult world. How many parents declare in frustration, "I just can't understand that child!" or "You are no child of mine!"? In self-defence, that child has travelled to a safe space within themselves, to his or her own foreign land. Persisting in this coping skill into adulthood, however, means selling himself or herself into slavery.

It is an all-too-common tragedy that many people live much of their lives exiled in these foreign lands within themselves. As they grow older, they develop more subtle and effective ways of acting out their pain through harmful words or actions. They are not true to themselves; their words say one thing, but the underlying message, portrayed by their body language and destructive behavioural patterns, says something else.

They may appear to be walking in step with the "drummer" – their parents, society, the church, or the community – but in reality they are following the beat of the little drummer boy or girl within. The beat of their broken heart is always in the background, deep in the roots of their being. Some may break step with society's accepted norms and become dysfunctional children who later develop into dysfunctional adults, alcoholics, overeaters, drug addicts. Some become criminals – angry, alienated people literally living in the foreign lands, the prisons, that our society has erected.

Many people are also imprisoned within their own broken hearts. Their life spirit is gone and they feel doomed. What hope can we offer them? Isaiah gives us a hint: "The spirit of the Lord GOD is upon me, because the LORD has anointed me; he has sent me to bring the good news to the oppressed, to bind up the brokenhearted, to proclaim liberty to the captives" (Isaiah 61:1). We have overlooked the challenge to preach the good news to the poor and to free the broken-hearted from the prisons within their own psyche; we must remember that we have the gifts and God's promise that he will guide us and set us free.

This insight has greatly energized me in the many years that I have committed myself to this work at Bountyfull. Helping someone enter into the sacred sanctuary of their own soul with gentleness and care is a deeply spiritual experience for me.

How do these pilgrims from foreign lands come to us, and who are they? They are people from a variety of situations who have finally realized that they can no longer tolerate the pain of their broken heart. They have coped or merely survived for many years, and have hidden the manifestations of pain and brokenness within the depths of their being. Some find a caring community, AA or another 12-step group, that leads them to us, while others are referred to us by their doctor.

This concept of foreign lands within is exemplified in the story of a young woman who was referred to me recently by her doctor. "Vicki" was helplessly locked into an addiction to prescription drugs – her only way of surviving the constant, hidden pain of her broken heart.

Vicki's Story: "Dark Blue"

For the past few years, "Vicki" had been struggling with repeated anxiety attacks and extreme depression. She had lost her job and was no longer able to work. For almost two years she had been seeing a psychiatrist, who had prescribed antidepressant medication and Valium to help her cope with the anxiety attacks. Her anxiety was heightened by his prognosis, which was that she would never be free of the anxiety attacks and would require the medication indefinitely. She told him that the medication had not worked for her and she felt like a zombie. Her doctor referred her to me to help her deal with her anxiety and the source of her depression.

Vicki, who was in her mid-30s, was filled with anxiety as she faced the prospect of looking at her story. She said her body felt very stiff; she had been considerably out of control because these moods of depression were like a "dark blue" feeling that enveloped her whole being. The numinous relationships within her broken heart became evident in the words she used and in the way her body was affected. When Vicki was apprehensive about this dark blue feeling, she seemed to sink more deeply into it and become overwhelmed by depression. These feelings further accentuated her anxiety because of her fear that something would cause it to happen again.

I set her at ease by assuring her that we would delve only as deep as she felt comfortable with. She liked the idea of tracing her story back to its roots, and of charting her story as we followed it. She felt this would help her discover where her depression and anxiety had originated.

When she was little, she had been very close to her father. She was his "special little girl." But that relationship soon ended because he was always fighting with her mother, who was mean and angry. The fights were so violent that they terrified Vicki, but she felt she could not turn to anyone for help. She vividly recalled her mother's loud, angry screaming. This recollection brought her back to her first conscious memory.

The family was driving to her grandmother's. Vicki's infant sister, Sherri, was in her car seat between Vicki and her brother. Vicki remembered her mother turning around from the front seat with a look of fear and terror in her eyes. She became hysterical and began screaming uncontrollably as she looked at little Sherri, who had turned a dark blue colour. The family had just arrived in the grandmother's driveway; they took the baby into the kitchen, put her on the table and did everything they could to revive her, but she died.

I asked Vicki what she did, how she handled the situation. She simply said, "I put it out of my mind. Even to this day, my brother and I live as though we never had a little sister, because she was never really part of our family; she lived for only six months."

In following her story, I helped her to discover when her anxiety attacks first began. Almost immediately she related them to an incident when she was about nine years old. She was playing peacefully at home when a dark blue car drove past with a young boy inside. At first Vicki could not discern how this incident had caused her anxiety. Then she realized that the driver, a boy about 16 years old, had awakened another memory for her. When she was four years old, she was molested by a babysitter who was about 16. Both her parents were out; she and her older brother were alone with the babysitter in the house. Her brother was asleep in his own room and Vicki had gotten up to go to the bathroom. The babysitter knew that Vicki had a sweet tooth and asked her if she wanted some candy. Innocently she accepted, but he would only give her the candy if she would allow him to fondle her. She was filled with great fear when he touched her and her body seemed to freeze and become stiff. She didn't know what to do and there was no one to turn to for help. She felt very frightened and alone.

On the chart we reviewed the source of her initial recollection of panic and anxiety when she was nine years old and became terrified by the blue car. It was then that she remembered that her father's car was blue also, though a lighter shade. This awakened the realization that the symbol of "blue" had a far deeper meaning for her than simply a blue car. She saw that the "dark blue" feeling of her overpowering depression had its roots in the terrifying screams of her mother when she saw little Sherri turn dark blue in death.

When Vicki was about 10, her parents separated. Her mother became extremely abusive towards her and would beat her severely at the slightest provocation. She felt that this might have been because she had always been "daddy's special little girl." Her mother had always resented their closeness and took out her anger at her husband on Vicki. This awareness helped Vicki get in touch with and own that early love she had for her father, whom she had seen only twice in over 30 years. In her session, she began to open her heart to him again and to find the strength within herself to let her mother go free. She added, "That explains why I have had so much trouble with my stomach this past year; I have had her in my gut all these years."

This awareness released her from her feelings of anxiety. She was later able to say that this session had given her an "objective awareness of where it all began and allows me to take control of my own life and not to feel helpless." With a great sense of relief, she finally knew where both her anxiety and depression came from. She concluded the session by saying, "I'm going to get off those pills and take back my own life. I will be a zombie no longer."

The Psyche is a Self-regulating System

I was excited when I first read Carl Jung's statement in *Analytical Psychology: Its Theory and Practice* that "the psyche is a self-regulating system due to a compensatory relationship between the unconscious and the conscious"

(New York: Random House, 1968, p. xv). This indicated to me that the psyche, like the body itself, is not only self-regulating, but it has its own God-given gifts of self-healing.

I was deeply impressed with this great mystery. As we observed in Vicki's story, by owning the messages that her pain and destructive behavioural patterns were giving her, she participated in the process of her own inner healing. Comprehending the hidden message from the unconscious is called "cognitive awareness."

As we followed Vicki's story I could sense the deep yearning within her to be freed from the darkness of her depression; her psyche graphically conveyed that message in the "dark blue" symbol that shrouded her soul. The cognitive awareness of what had happened in her own life story allowed Vicki, who was overwhelmed and depressed, to reawaken her spirit and to co-operate with the healing power of God to set herself free from oppression.

In Vicki's story, we saw clearly that her dysfunctional behavioural patterns compensated for her pain and carried a message beyond themselves. These messages conveyed the compensatory relationship between her unconscious and her conscious self. The breakthrough she experienced in her session made tangible the wealth of the mystery of accessing these messages from the unconscious. Once again, I was amazed to discover that deep within the broken heart lie the answers that are needed for release from the prison of pain and denial and, at the same time, for the direction for healing.

Discerning the "Vibes"
of Compensatory Relationships

Mysteriously, our wrongs are our own unique form of portraying the compensatory relationship from our unconscious to our conscious awareness. We can only become aware of the presence of these relationships when we are attuned to the messages and the energy that they carry.

In every session I feel a thrill as people begin to tell their story. I do not think with my head alone; I listen with my heart. As Matthew reminds us in his gospel, in order to grasp the message that the spirit is trying to convey, we must learn to see with our eyes, and hear with our ears, and understand with our hearts:

> "For this people's heart has grown dull....
> so that they might not look with their eyes,
> and listen with their ears,
> and understand with their heart – and turn
> and I would heal them."

> (*Matthew 13:13-16, quoting Isaiah*)

The clues to the root of the pain are harboured within our personal unconscious or our shadow, to which we commit the memory of that denied pain, and can be discerned only if we are attuned to the energy and the dynamism in the feeling-toned phrases and deviant behavioural patterns, which reveal that loving hearts have turned into hearts of stone.

Understanding that the psyche is a self-regulating system, I am always challenged to be sensitive to, and to attempt to discern, the numinous, spiritual reality of these compensatory relationships. (Relationships in and of themselves cannot be discerned, but their spiritual aspect can be.) The dynamism and energy they carry are manifested in the *dynamic feeling-toned phrases* and *symbols* that characterize a person's life. This realization was a real breakthrough for me in my quest to help people discern the hidden cause of their dysfunctional behavioural patterns.

COMPENSATORY RELATIONSHIP

At Bountyfull we see life as a *story*. We do not focus on the *problem*. We trace the feelings, behavioural patterns from present trauma back the pathways of the past, by discerning **The Compensatory Relationship** between the unconscious and the conscious.

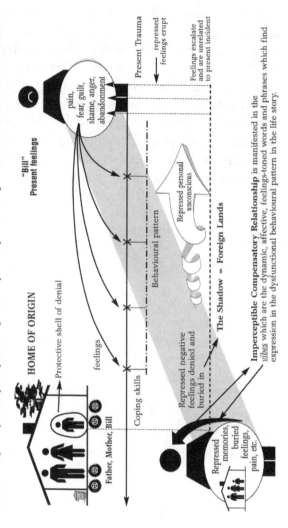

These are not visible, discernible, concrete realities, because by definition behavioural patterns are experiential. I believe that these mysterious, energy-filled compensatory relationships can be discerned in the energy field around them. In this way, the inaccessible reality of these relationships begins to become manifest and almost tangible in the aura surrounding them.

We pick up these inaudible yet real vibes that emanate from the painful messages that these compensatory relationships carry. We see and sense in aggressive, angry, violent behaviour and words messages that mask the pain of a broken heart. These numinous relationships can be grasped when we comprehend how they affect our bodies, our soma, as I indicated in the fourth quadrant of the little toy man (see Chapter 2).

Just as an electric current has an energy field that surrounds a conduit, relationships are like electrical wires that carry the energy-filled current within them. These vibes surround the dynamic feeling-toned phrases and destructive behavioural patterns that are charged with meaning and power.

If someone has buried a feeling of rejection, pain or abuse and attempts to deny it, the relationship between that denied feeling and the conscious awareness becomes almost electrified. By that I mean that the person becomes extremely touchy and even explosive when another person inadvertently touches that buried pain. This aura is visible in the very sensitive feelings of fear, guilt and shame that surround that relationship with our unconscious. The power is usually negative, and is expressed in a variety of negative phrases and actions. You can sense the vibes in the words themselves, especially those that carry negative messages of pain and brokenness.

In this way I understood the deep meaning of the psychological term "affective feeling-toned phrases" or "dynamic feeling-toned phraseology." I began to discern how words affected the body, telling the story of a heart that was broken and deadened by pain. I cherished the words as such and was impressed by their power to convey the painful experiences of our lives. Often, when I listen to people's stories, words such as "abandoned," "terrified," "sacrificed" and "rejected" are used over and over again. The fear and anxiety that these words convey becomes almost palpable. These dynamic feeling-toned phrases and the symbolic language of our words or actions can guide us to the buried roots of our childhood pain.

Once we are aware of what we are searching for, these "spirit killers" are only too evident, because they are the "problems" that have rendered us helpless. We are not consciously aware that they are the cause of our loss of power and energy; we are aware only of their effect. The gift of discerning the root of our buried pain is that it reveals the source of the "exact nature of our wrongs," as the 5th step puts it. We must honestly face the parts of our stories that bear so much pain to discover what happened in our lives.

This hidden dynamic is revealed in Willie's story. Listen with your heart as we follow the painful pathway to his past. It is truly a journey in faith.

Willie's Story: "Run, Willie! Run!"

"Willie" was referred to me by a counsellor in the alcoholic program, although his current problem was not alcohol as such. He had been dry for a number of years and lived a very private life; in fact, he lived almost like a hermit. He began to question his inability to relate to other people, his isolated existence and his recurring bouts of anger, although they have never been excessive. He had dedicated his life to the church, but wanted to be excused from that obligation because it put too much stress on him to preach, speak up and guide others in how to live.

As he looked back over his story, he saw that this tension and stress brought on his alcoholism. He had not realized before that he was dependent on alcohol as a way to cope with stress. In searching his story for times of stress and anger, and especially as he traced it back to his early childhood, he said he had very few memories. Laughingly he mentioned that there was only one that stood out for him. When he was four years old or so, he and his six-year-old brother, Johnnie, whom he greatly admired, both had tonsillitis. In those days, over 65 years ago, many children had their tonsils removed at home. His mother called the doctor in; Willie remembered Johnnie being placed on the kitchen table and put to sleep. Willie didn't know what it was all about and was told to leave the room. He sneaked back in to see what was going on and was shocked to see blood everywhere – bowls of blood. He felt the panic in the room from both the doctor and his mother, although she seemed to be the calmer of the two. The artery was finally clamped and the bleeding stopped. But while he was there in the kitchen, Johnnie woke up and said in a whisper, "Run, Willie! Run!" Willie didn't know what he meant, but he didn't want to leave his brother. He wanted to stay with him and protect him, but his mother took Willie out of the room.

As Willie told that story, he reluctantly got in touch with the anger he felt towards the doctor, and even towards his mother, though he felt she had been trying to protect him. He didn't remember clearly what happened after that, but was startled to recall that he was next in line, that he, too, was placed on the kitchen table to have his tonsils removed. All he could remember was the terrible fear – not so much for himself as for his brother. His mother tried to assure him that Johnnie was fine and that everything would be fine for him as well.

As Willie began to look at his story as it unfolded, he realized that very early in his life he became a loner. At first he worked with his father and brother, but then he became a tradesman in his own right. He never found his work meaningful and had always felt drawn to the priesthood instead, where he felt, in his own words, that would be "safe." But as the years progressed, he experienced great stress, particularly when he was asked to preach. More recently he noticed how easily upset he would get when he was ignored, even in simple situations, and especially in any line-up, such as at the grocery store, when he felt that he was "next in line." He was irritated if people did not notice him or demonstrate care or concern for him, and would want to leave the situation immediately.

As Willie reflected on all this, it suddenly struck him that all his life he had been running, running to find a "safe" place. When faced with any form of stress, he would immediately try to escape, either through alcohol or, more recently, in turning to the monastery. He now knew that this propensity to flee to a safe place had its roots in that original loving phrase spoken in the weak voice of his older brother, whom he almost lost. He could still hear the words clearly: "Run, Willie! Run!"

Our Deeper Craving

When we are driven by alcohol or chemical addictions, we can become lost and can sink into despair. Often we think the source of the problem is only the chemical addiction, because these addictions wreak great havoc in personal lives and relationships. Chemical addictions can create such physical cravings that the body is almost torn apart unless there is some form of detoxification done. Joining a self-help group such as a 12-step program can give people with addictions relief and a sense of serenity through the confessional approach in a caring community and the many guidelines that the program provides to help people overcome dysfunctional behaviours. But while slogans such as "One day at a time" and "Let go and let God" offer helpful guidance in times of crisis, they do not address the buried pain that leads to the addiction. I believe that a deeper craving exists that most people are totally unaware of; it is buried within the shadow of our repressed pain. People who do not address this deeper craving may adjust their behavioural patterns but still not achieve the serenity they seek. Many clients have acknowledged when they come for a session, "I have been dry and clean for so many years, but I feel like a dry drunk. There is something that still drives me and I have no serenity or peace."

In treating a compulsive alcoholic, the genius of Jung's insight was the awareness that this devastating chemical craving was, as he explains in *Pass It On*, "the equivalent on a low level, of his spiritual thirst for wholeness, which in medieval terminology is union with God" (New York: Alcoholics Anonymous, 1984, pp. 383-385).

The deeper, underlying craving is that spiritual craving for wholeness and for union with God. Without a union with God, we seek to be united with various substitutes in the hope that something or someone can fulfill our yearning for wholeness and fill the void within. People and relationships can bring us a degree of love and fulfillment, but the depth we all crave is to be consciously connected to our inner selves and to our creator.

Cravings for chemicals and other substitutes can be overcome only by honesty and openness, by becoming consciously aware of the root and cause of our pain, and by turning it over to God, whatever we understand God to be. The approach we use at Bountyfull allows people not only to be free to discover for themselves the hidden cause of their pain, but to move beyond that childlike fear and take responsibility as an adult, speaking openly and freely to God and naming the healing they so greatly desire. As we saw in Willie's story, there can be no healing unless the hidden dynamic that has caused a loss of spirit or a deep sense of depression is unearthed.

Willie learned that this one traumatic incident held many messages for him, and he has committed himself to discover what the other messages mean in his life story. In this way he became a partner in his own healing. In his prayer for healing, he could now become consciously aware of what he was asking of God, rather than being the angry, petulant child who simply threw it all back at God, expecting God to heal all his hurts.

I hear Christ's comforting phrase: "I no longer call you servants, I call you friends" (John 15:15). This energizing message reminds us that we move from being helpless victims to becoming people who walk into a fullness of life with God.

Willie lived the life of a loner; for safety, in his alcoholism, he ran from all responsibility and contact with people. I helped him see that the reason he held onto that one memory of his childhood was because it was the "negative payoff." In holding onto that negative, frightening incident, he was reconnecting with his loving brother, whom he wanted to protect and defend. His brother's dynamic feeling-toned phrase – "Run, Willie! Run!" – had an energy that became the symbol of Willie's life. When he understood what his symbol stood for, he saw that he was no longer running from pain, but striving to reconnect with his brother, to whom he felt so grateful.

As we saw in the above case, these messages of compensatory relationships are not easily discernible. They are expressed in distorted forms – not only in words as such, but in painful behavioural patterns or violent outbursts from within our being – that are closely related to the confusing messages that arise from our unconscious in our dreams.

Symbol: A Waking Dream

The language of dreams is extremely confusing and complex because it is expressed in symbolic forms that emerge from that dark world of the unconscious and are unique to the dreamer. Only he or she holds the key to its meaning. Yet, in dream analysis, these hidden messages can be revealed.

In our work at Bountyfull, I treat people's dysfunctional behavioural pattern and the symbolic expression of their buried pain as a "waking dream." The people who come to me are often not in touch with themselves as they live through the experiences. They may become carried away by the intensity of their feeling and appear to be living in something like a fantasy world. Unknowingly, they can become trapped in prisons of their own making. They become locked into a pattern, acting out of their shadow from the buried pain.

The confusing messages of the waking dream are very personal to each of us, as "Run, Willie! Run!" was to Willie. A symbol can be as difficult to access as a dream itself, because the messages are a spontaneous creation of the unconscious mind. Willie's symbol is unique to him and therefore is almost the signature of his life story.

A symbol is evoked by the pain and is expressed in the compensatory relationship between the unconscious and the conscious. It becomes expressed in a word, phrase, action or behavioural pattern that depicts the very root of the problem. The symbol points to the past hidden experience, and is visible in the present dysfunction. It is also the bridge between the pain of the past experience and the future healing.

The symbol is a window onto the soul. For this reason, it is important for those who are accompanying people with past hurts to see through the symbol of behavioural dysfunction to the hidden root of the problem and sense the beating of the broken heart beneath it all. Willie, for example, had been treated several times in residential alcoholic treatment centres, but had never been able to overcome the deep, driving compulsion to run, either by using alcohol or by escaping into some form of isolation.

Symbols have the mysterious power to simultaneously indicate the root of the problem, the present coping skill, and the direction for healing. In other words, a symbol indicates what must be released or let go of in order to allow the spirit to come alive once again.

Seeing the function of a symbol made me realize that there were tangible clues to this mysterious depth within our being. The beauty of the clues is that they are the unique expressions of our own creation. This insight provides a way of probing the shadows of those protective shells in which the spirit has been entombed.

As children, we deny our fear and our pain by putting on the mask of socially acceptable behavioural patterns. As the song says, we are "laughing on the outside, and crying on the inside." This life pattern eventually becomes second nature. Healing can be achieved only when we become aware that our present problems have their roots in early childhood or past experience.

In order to comprehend how a person can be bound by some unconscious power buried in their shadow and live in a "foreign land," let's listen to Rose's story.

Rose's Story: Bound in a Foreign Land

When "Rose" came to me, she was dealing with a long history of severe depression that often rendered her unable to cope in her position as an accountant for a large company. She felt powerless and had decided to quit her job.

I began with her present concern, telling her that we would follow the pathway of her story to help discover the source of her depression. I said that it is difficult to discern the root of depression, because often the cause is repressed or buried anger. This anger is so cleverly denied, most people cannot identify it.

As we traced her recurring bouts of depression and her loss of energy and purpose in life, she returned to a time when she was a little girl. Almost in passing, and somewhat embarrassed, she said the strongest memory that came to mind was a conversation that her aunt and mother had about her. She recalled a strong feeling of shame and almost denial as she remembered what her aunt said: "This child must be retarded, because she's always playing behind closed doors."

All her life Rose had carried within herself the shameful stigma of being "retarded," but she continually repressed these feelings. Even as an adult, when she could not comprehend or succeed at a task, she felt "retarded." She would lose all her energy and hope and slip into another depression without knowing why.

Reflecting on her story, Rose said that she had lived in constant fear when she witnessed her parents fighting. Her mother hated liquor; when her father would come home drunk, they would start fighting and yelling. Rose, filled with fear, always wanted to protect her father. Above all, she wanted to make her family look like a "decent" family. More than once, she was filled with terror as she heard her father threaten to cut his throat with the sharp straight razor he had always used for shaving.

Dad would say, "I'll go to the kitchen and cut my throat." I'd beg him not to do that. Mom would simply say, "He'll never do that, it's just a threat," but I never knew because I believed him. I was afraid of losing him, because I was always so special to him. When I was a child he had bought me a special suit of overalls which my mother would not let me wear because I was a girl. Dad was always special to me. I wanted him to be there for me, and I felt she didn't care if Dad lived or died. Dad would take off in anger, leave the house and violently slam the door and go down to join the fellows at the pub. I missed dad and was sorry to see him angry and have to leave home. I wanted to be close to him and to get out of Mom's sight. In my fear I unconsciously did what he did, I "hid behind closed doors."

Rose would hide behind the kitchen door and play quietly there. It was a safe place for her, away from the turmoil and out of her mother's sight. She recalled that she would return to her safe place every time her father left the house in anger and slammed the door behind him.

She discovered with great relief how clever her childlike game was. It was her safe place; in her childish

71

mind, it gave her the feeling that she was connected to her father, whom she loved. Unconsciously she had fled to the prison of her foreign land behind closed doors. She realized that there was a message both for her and for her father, but she never saw that the strongest message was to her mother and aunt. The message to her father was that she wanted to be connected to him because she loved him. So she played his game, but while he could escape from the house, she had to stay inside the house.

Rose wasn't aware until our session that she had been angry at her mother all her life for accepting her aunt's labelling her as "retarded." She was never free to express that anger because she feared she would lose the only contact she had with her mother, whom she really did love. When she was a child, she cut herself off from her mother by playing behind closed doors in order to cope with the pain of fear and rejection. Later in life, in her anger she literally lived out her mother's condemnation of her by slipping into depression as a way of punishing and unconsciously blaming her. She was startled to discover that her successive depressions were a more sophisticated way of being cut off from her mother, of finding a safe place, by being completely out of reach. In our session I sensed her joy when she discovered that in her depression she had created within herself that safe place behind closed doors. Once she realized that, she peacefully reconnected with her father and renewed her love for him. This gave her the strength to stand up to her mother and her aunt and, as an adult, to give the fear of being a "retarded child" back to them and set both of them free. Doing so allowed her to love her mother freely without being angry about the stigma she had carried all her life.

This past year, Rose has been free of her depression and filled with energy to explore a new and challenging career. Amazingly, she has volunteered to work part-time with depressed and disadvantaged people.

The release that Rose experienced reminds me of the woman in Luke's gospel who had been crippled for 18 years. She was bent over and unable to stand up straight. Jesus said to the Pharisees, "You hypocrites! ...ought not this woman, a daughter of Abraham whom Satan has bound for eighteen long years, be set free from this bondage...?" (Luke 13:10-17)

No matter how long a person has been enslaved, freedom is possible. Sometimes we lose sight of the phenomenal spirit within us that brings us energy and new life, but when we are deeply rooted within ourselves we can truly be set free.

The Mystery of the Broken Heart

In early childhood, when we live amid fear and pain, or experience rejection or violence, we flee as Rose did to foreign lands within ourselves; we live in lands of fear, rejection and powerlessness. In order to cope, we create a persona, a socially acceptable self. We learn to speak and act with a language of anger, violence, resentment, deception or depression.

Like Rose, we know we are controlled by a power beyond ourselves, as if we have been cast into slavery. In exile, we yearn to come back to our homeland, our real selves.

The constant challenge at Bountyfull is to detect the effects of a crushed spirit in those who come to us for healing. We must be sensitive to the broken heart that yearns to be free and to be healed. Our approach allows people to enter into the depths of their misery and pain, while at the same time giving them the tools to understand their whole story. With their belief in God, they can release the chains that bind them.

4

Hearts of Stone

I will sprinkle clean water upon you, and you shall be clean
from all your uncleannesses, and from all your idols I will
cleanse you. A new heart I will give you, and a new spirit I
will put within you; and I will remove from your body the
heart of stone and give you a heart of flesh.

(Ezekiel 36:25-27)

Every human being is looking for love. This is a
fundamental yearning within us: when we are not
loved freely and naturally, we may feel rejected, develop
low self-esteem, or carry a burden of guilt or shame. Many
people have walked through our doors at Bountyfull
carrying so much pain within their broken spirits that it
shows in their very bodies. They emanate messages of
discomfort, antagonism, guilt, shame, fear or utter
powerlessness.

All of us use a variety of coping skills to deny our
own pain and brokenness; generally speaking, we do this
unconsciously. We all tend, in one way or another, to
create our own prisons and live as unwilling captives
within their confining walls. These prison walls, this
shell, this hardness of heart allows us to swallow the pain,

to deny it and to put on the mask of a happy face, or of a driven person, or to devise whatever form of coping skill we choose. We can become the most skilled manipulators or con artists. Sadly, we not only manipulate others, but ourselves as well. We try to create a fantasy of who we would like to be; we put on our mask, our persona, our socially acceptable self.

Our Childhood Perception

When we encounter trauma as children, we may experience a range of negative feelings. These feelings result from our perception of what has happened. When we are helpless, dependent children, we need adults to care for us and make us feel safe. If adults let us down, we find a way to do the job ourselves. If we have no one to turn to for help, or if we are unable to express our feelings, we try to make sense of the situation and pick up ways of coping from those around us. Children often believe that a difficult situation is somehow their fault. The fear and pain that result from this guilt can be heartbreaking.

Hearts of Stone: That Protective Shell

The impenetrable protective shell we build around ourselves, which is formed out of the childhood perception, functions in two ways: it protects us from further pain, but this may render us powerless, immobile, depressed and ultimately helpless when we unconsciously act out of that hidden pain. The child puts up the protective shell to defend the self from the significant

LOSS OF LIFE POWER

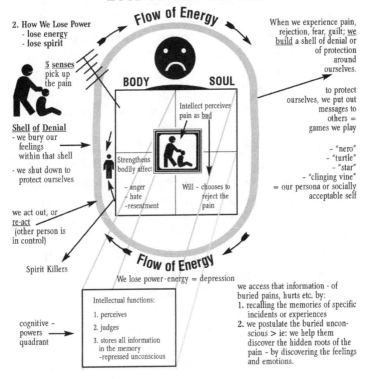

Flow of Energy

2. How We Lose Power
   - lose energy
   - lose spirit

When we experience pain, rejection, fear, guilt; <u>we build</u> a shell of denial or of protection around ourselves.

<u>5 senses</u> pick up the pain

BODY   **SOUL**

Intellect perceives pain as <u>bad</u>

to protect ourselves, we put out messages to others = games we play

<u>Shell of Denial</u>
- we bury our feelings within that shell

- we shut down to protect ourselves

Strengthens bodily affect

- "nero"
- "turtle"
- "star"
- "clinging vine"
= our persona or socially acceptable self

- anger
- hate
- resentment

Will - chooses to reject the pain

we act out, or <u>re-act</u> (other person is in control)

Spirit Killers

Flow of Energy

We lose power - energy = depression

we access that information - of buried pains, hurts etc. by:
1. recalling the memories of specific incidents or experiences
2. we postulate the buried unconscious > ie: we help them discover the hidden roots of the pain - by discovering the feelings and emotions.

cognitive - powers quadrant

Intellectual functions:

1. perceives

2. judges

3. stores all information in the memory
   - repressed unconscious

other who inflicted the original pain, and to send messages that convey to others the child's pain due to the loss of love or the anger harboured within his or her heart. Our loving hearts of flesh can become hearts of stone when survival techniques or coping skills, with constant repetition, develop into behavioural patterns.

In the diagram below, the little toy man helps us to comprehend how the child is locked within that protective shell. The first stage shows how the child deadens and buries the pain by locking it within the shell. The messages that the child unconsciously puts out depict the various stages he or she develops to cope with that hidden pain and protect him or herself from further punishment or rejection. Their dysfunctional behavior may give very strong messages to others, such as "This is my land and you shall not cross these boundaries."

Our shell can be as sturdy as a concrete wall of silence, or as fragile as a glass cage.

One client recently told me he survives by living in a cage made of bullet-proof dark glass that allows him to see out, but does not allow others to see him. He has a desperate need to be loved, but he keeps others on the outside, behind this glass wall. Before our session, he never realized that people could see his wall, although they did not understand the game he was playing.

People can become touchy about these coping skills and behavioural patterns, sending out threatening messages like arrows. They often fear that if they give up these behavioural patterns, they will not survive; these games have become almost second nature to them and they know no other way to live.

PROCESS: Trace the **feelings** to a significant experience in which this, or these feeling(s) were dominant.
Then, discover our dysfunctional behaviour patterns and trace them to their source, the roots of our behaviour.

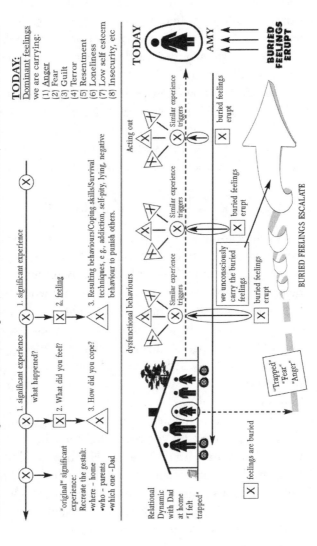

TODAY:

Dominant feelings
we are carrying:
(1) Anger
(2) Fear
(3) Guilt
(4) Terror
(5) Resentment
(6) Loneliness
(7) Low self esteem
(8) Insecurity, etc

1. significant experience

2. feeling

3. Resulting behaviours/Coping skills/Survival
techniques, e.g., addiction, self-pity, lying, negative
behaviour to punish others.

dysfunctional behaviours

Acting out

Similar experience
triggers

buried feelings
erupt

we unconsciously
carry the buried
feelings

BURIED FEELINGS ESCALATE

TODAY

AMY

BURIED
FEELINGS
ERUPT

1. significant experience

what happened?

2. What did you feel?

3. How did you cope?

"original" significant
experience:
Recreate the gestalt:
• where – home
• who – parents
• which one –Dad

Relational
Dynamic
with Dad
at home
"I felt
trapped"

feelings are buried

"Trapped"
"Fear"
"Anger"

When we can no longer live with the pain of the guilt or shame that we have buried or denied, this fantasy world is no longer effective. We may develop deviant behavioural patterns to seek attention or to make a statement to the world around us. Soon we are trapped in a snare of our own making.

Jane's story shows how children unconsciously form their own unique coping skills that create in them a heart of stone. Their hope is to be free of pain, but almost always, the coping skills they devise lock them into defiant and destructive behavioural patterns.

Jane's Story: "The Pit of My Stomach"

A 40-year-old woman, "Jane," had become a chronic overeater and at times was completely powerless over her craving for food. She had come to Bountyfull once before to deal with her anger towards her workaholic husband, whom she felt made unreasonable demands of her. One morning she phoned me quite distraught about her intense feelings of anger. She felt powerless – she had shouted at her seven-year-old daughter and upset her without knowing where the anger had come from. She wanted healing.

Jane was overwhelmed by her many responsibilities: she cared full-time for their disabled son, their seven-year-old daughter and their home. Her husband had an office in the basement; at times he would demand that Jane come downstairs to help him when she already had her own work to do and could not leave her son unattended. Even more upsetting for Jane, though, was her terrible fear that as soon as she was down there, her husband would "ask more of her than she was capable of giving." This fear gave her an awful, sick feeling in the "pit of her stomach." This frequent scenario would always result in an argument.

It was following just such an argument that Jane phoned me and began to recount her frustrations about falling back into her anger and her addiction to food. In our telephone conversation, as she followed her feelings, she became aware of a forgotten childhood memory. This memory awakened an uncontrollable fear within her.

When she was five, she would be sent to her parents' bedroom for an afternoon nap. When her father came home from work, he would lie down with her. He would begin by just offering affection and cuddling close to her, but then would abuse her. She did what he wanted in order to please him, because she wanted him to love her, but she always felt he wanted more from her than she could give. Her fear made her angry and produced a sick feeling in the pit of her stomach.

During our telephone session Jane said, "Somehow I knew that what was happening with Dad didn't feel right. It just felt wrong. I even asked Dad if he was sure it was okay. I decided to stay there with Dad, even though I felt it was wrong. I wanted him to love me. I felt so guilty. I knew I couldn't tell Mom; she already hated Dad and I really wanted her to love him, and I really wanted her to love me, too."

Jane tried to please her father to keep his love; she also tried to gain her mother's love by hiding her own guilt, fear and pain. In her childhood perception, she felt that the abuse was her own fault.

In order to cope, she buried or stuffed all her feelings into the pit of her stomach. The only way she could kill the pain of that sick feeling was to fill her stomach with something that made her feel good. As a child, she unconsciously developed a behavioural pattern of eating cookies, which became her coping skill; it gave her the ability to suffer through her pain and find some comfort. Anytime she had that terrible feeling in the pit of her stomach, she would eat cookies. As she was speaking to me on the phone, Jane realized with amazement that the nearly empty package of cookies on her kitchen counter, the same cookies she kept in the cupboard and ate in secret, were the brand Dad's Cookies.

This awareness gave her some insight into the source of her uncontrollable urge to eat cookies. The cookies were a coping skill she used to deaden her intolerable pain. By following back her story to the original root of the pain, she discovered she had been entombed all her life in a prison of guilt and fear, because she had been tricked by her father into agreeing to let him abuse her. Jane knew as a child that she had to be quiet and not make a noise, for fear that her mother would discover what was going on. As a result, Jane felt that if she said anything she would be guilty both of getting her father into trouble and of doing something she felt was wrong.

In her present situation, Jane was able to see how her fear that her husband would ask her "to do more than she was capable of" hooked her into those childhood feelings of guilt and fear. As an adult, when circumstances between Jane and her husband touched that buried guilt and fear, Jane would become overwhelmed with anger. The invasion of those buried feelings caused Jane to erupt at her husband. She would leave the basement office in a rage, go upstairs and eat cookies.

Jane was not capable of responding as an adult to these incidents. Unknowingly, she had held on to her parents all these years by seeing herself as the problem and remaining locked in her negative feelings of guilt and fear. She had spent her life trying to fix the problem to gain their approval. Finally, she realized that the problem was theirs, not hers. The guilt she carried was not hers, either. She had taken on their guilt and carried it all her life as a means of staying connected to them. (This is what I describe as the negative payoff.)

No longer motivated by the guilt or fear of that sick feeling in the pit of her stomach, she was able to accept her parents in all their brokenness, and set them free. She accepted herself as the innocent five-year-old child that she had been, and regained her sense of self. She was thereby freed of her compulsion to eat cookies. Her overwhelming anger towards her husband was relieved, and she became free to respond to him as an adult woman.

The Negative Payoff

We can see from Jane's story the wealth of meaning in an unconscious coping skill that develops into a compulsion that is ultimately destructive.

We unconsciously choose to maintain negative behavioural patterns because they are familiar and therefore comforting. As we saw in Jane's story, the comfort is short-lived. The negative payoff remains strongly impressed in our memories, affecting both our psyches and our bodies and bringing with it a residual feeling of the original pain of loss. The negative memory we carry is always connected to some significant other, such as a parent, a sibling or another caring person; alternatively, the memory may be connected to someone who inflicted great pain that took our spirit away.

This is the key to the negative payoff. It is an unconscious way of maintaining contact with some significant other whose love we greatly desired or with someone we hoped we could change if they did not love us the way we felt we needed to be loved. They inflicted a sense of rejection or guilt; unconsciously, we nurture both the guilt and the pain of rejection because these are the negative conduits to that early connection with that significant other. Often, without knowing it, we transfer that source of our longing to someone else who represents or has similarities to the person we are seeking to contact.

The Shadow of a Significant Other

The difficulty in uprooting or eradicating the negative payoff in compulsive addictions or behavioural patterns is that they are accompanied by an almost immediate sense of gratification and release. The more we are addicted to alcohol, drugs, sex or food, the quicker the body reacts; hence, we experience a "glow" or a "high" almost immediately. This is a false sense of release, however, for the current state is worse than the last. It plunges us into deeper darkness and depression as soon as the chemical, or whatever we have chosen to compensate for the pain, wears off.

The same is true of all dysfunctional behavioural patterns. They can bring an immediate sense of release and gratification, particularly when we feel that the coping skill has in some way gotten back at someone, although all we have really done is widen the gulf. Eventually we realize that we are unconsciously getting back at some "shadow" or residual memory of a significant other, and the problem accelerates. We unwittingly create situations that have all the dynamics of the original trauma, and transfer all our indignation and pain from the past onto the "aggressor." We recreate the repressed memory because it is familiar, and unconsciously experience the negative payoff, the sense of satisfaction that comes from expressing our negative feelings.

The Development of Our Persona

Behavioural patterns become what we term our persona, our socially acceptable self. This persona can also be described, in Jung's terms, as an "alter ego" – something that is not truly ourselves or the free expression of our own person. The persona is the compilation of all the behavioural patterns and coping skills that we create in order to survive in the midst of pain and rejection. As children we develop our coping skills in order to be accepted, but as we move to adulthood they become more sophisticated, more dysfunctional. We justify our actions, saying that someone else is to blame or that we have no other way to survive. As we grow older, these behavioural patterns that helped us survive as children can become addictions or compulsions and take away our freedom.

Doug's story shows very clearly how clever and creative a child can be in developing coping skills. These coping skills enabled him to survive in an impossible situation and at the same time sent out a message to his parents. Immediately after our session, Doug slipped out to his car and from memory recounted his story and the insights he had gained during the session. Here is his story, in his own words.

Doug's Story: From Pranks to Booze

My father and mother: In their relationship, my father was the subservient underdog; he never stood up for himself in conflict situations. My mother was the opposite: a domineering symbol of the establishment rules, regulations, control, consequences and power.

As a teenage boy, my pranks of building bombs, building a radio transmitter to jam broadcasting stations, and so on, was me breaking out of my shell of insecurity, shyness, inferiority, worry, self-consciousness, loneliness. It was *me showing my father* to stand up for himself and not to hide and sulk by going into the garden to pick stones out of the soil for hours on end, or stand for countless hours on a deserted beach, fishing, because he could not stand up to my mother and needed to get out and away from it all. It was also *me showing my mother* that I was breaking out of the shell that I had built around me from an early age from her controlling me and the whole family (making all the decisions and consequences).

At age 21 when I left home for university, I first discovered alcohol, and I took to it like a duck to water. Booze took over from bombs; with it I could break out of my shell. It gave me power, control, freedom, confidence, self-assurance, lack of inhibitions and self-consciousness, self-esteem, lack of worry and anxiety. I could now relate with others on an equal basis in any social situation (until I got completely inebriated).

Robbing police stations and other wild pranks was *me showing the world* and myself that I had broken free of my mother's control (and my protective shell) by rebelling against authority, laws, rules and regulations, and *me showing my dad* that he should stand up for himself against my mother's control, rules, power and authority.

Supporting the underdog and taking the opposite side of any discussion or argument throughout most of my life was because my father never stood up for himself so I was doing it for him and showing him what to do.

Today: By giving up and moving on, I am telling my parents that I am free of my mother's control and my father's lack of spunk in handling his situation, and that I am finally breaking out of the shell that controlled me (without the use of pranks, bombs, booze, etc.) through recognizing why I did the things I did. Until now, I could not understand why I did them.

I have given up my guilt over "Holly" (as I know she would want me to) for the many things I did wrong in my marriage. I want to tell her how much I love her and how I trusted and respected her and her abilities, but that I am now moving on and will always love her.

I can now come alive with my own many abilities that, until now, have been controlled by the hangovers from my past. I can take control back of my own spirit and power and lead a better, more productive, happier and more fulfilling life.

Doug's story indicates how his coping skills progressed to the degree that they became more sophisticated, moving from childhood pranks into compulsive addictions that resulted in a major inability to face his life as an adult and ultimately brought him to powerlessness.

Stages in the Development of Coping Skills

Over the years I have formulated an outline of the progressive stages of coping skills I have uncovered in people's stories:

1. People-pleasing
2. Reacting to get attention
3. Finding means to deaden the pain
4. Unconsciously blaming and attacking the significant other
5. Living the victim role
6. Completely disowning the significant other

You will notice that each of these coping skills or survival techniques send out positive or negative messages to that significant other. Unknowingly, through each of these coping skills, children give their power away to the other person; hence, they lose their own power or life spirit.

When I say that they have lost power, I mean that they no longer act freely, but react to that other person in anger, frustration or resentment or with violent and, ultimately, self-destructive behaviours. Let's explore each stage of the coping skills.

Stage 1: People-pleasing

When we feel we have lost the love of someone whom we deeply respect and greatly need, we develop people-pleasing skills in order to regain that love. We will do anything, regardless of the cost to ourselves, to overcome that loss or that sense of guilt.

As we saw in Jane's story, regardless of the pain that she feared would recur, she was willing to do anything to retain her father's love. She unconsciously gave all her power to her father, in the hope that he would accept and love her.

Let us also follow the progression of these coping skills in "Ann's" story, as she tells us: "I tried so hard to be good when I was growing up. To keep the peace, I put myself and my own needs last, to the extent that I made every attempt not to have any needs, or at least not to let them show."

Stage 2: Reacting to get attention

If people-pleasing does not work, then we devise means or schemes to at least get the attention, if not the love, of the other person. We react to the negative feedback we have received in order to find a way to compensate for the pain we feel. We begin to attract attention by developing negative behavioural patterns to upset the other person. We become disobedient, or blatantly break rules as a means of getting back at them.

Ann continues with her story, "Bit by bit I gave up trying to please. I began stealing at seven and took up drinking at fourteen. I began to skip classes and by the time I was sixteen rarely went to school at all. I remember one thing that really bothered Mum was that whenever she ranted abuse at me, I would just pass out; faint and keel right over. Boy, that got her going. It makes me smile to myself yet."

Stage 3: Deadening the pain

In our loneliness and pain we reach out to whatever will help to release us, or at least bring comfort. We develop skills to compensate for our need by satisfying our appetites for food, alcohol, sex, or whatever we may choose.

Ultimately, if we endlessly feed these appetites, we become prisoners of addictions and compulsions, driven by an ever-growing need to be satiated. Rather than hurting others by our negative behavioural pattern, we wreak destruction on ourselves. We use our bodies to send messages to our significant others from childhood; even if they are dead, we carry their memories and all the surrounding feelings that have been a source of difficulty in our lives. Like Jane, we unconsciously transfer these feelings to some unsuspecting person to whom we now direct our unspoken message.

Ann tells us, "When I was young I stole money to buy candy and constantly read romance comics, which my father had forbidden. As a teenager I read compulsively, learned to drink and slept; anything to kill the pain."

Stage 4: Blaming and attacking the significant other

Now that we have convinced ourselves that our current behaviour is not our fault, but the significant other's, we unconsciously absolve ourselves from all responsibility for our actions.

At Bountyfull, we have worked with many women who have worked as prostitutes a block away from us. This dynamic of blaming the significant other is often acted out unconsciously when a woman enters a life of prostitution. One young woman told me that every time she seduced a man, she called him "Daddy." Whenever she could, she would humiliate or punish the man she had chosen to replace her father.

Ann states, "I drank and when I was sixteen, I started having sex with boys I didn't know, or didn't like, to get back at my mother. As an adult I raged at my children and drank with impunity. 'They' made me the way I am; how could I help it?"

Stage 5: Living the victim role

If the other person does not accept blame, we will try to make them feel guilty by playing the victim, by calling attention to our pain. This allows us to wallow in the pain of the hurt child; it is the negative pay-off. We can take this to extremes and develop various forms of self-mutilation, and even attempt suicide. Unknowingly, we become the victims of our own games.

Jane lived the victim role by being constantly overworked. She took on her husband's requests or demands and either pushed herself to please him, or reacted angrily at his expectations.

Ann recalls, "Nobody understood. When my brother tried to talk to me about how I was neglecting my children, I wailed that he didn't understand. I was either raging or depressed. I left my children alone, screamed and yelled and hit them. If anyone tried to make me see sense, they didn't understand. It was different for me. I had such a sense of entitlement I nearly drowned in it."

Stage 6: Disowning the significant other

When we become aware that the victim game is not working – that our pain is still unheard and our broken heart is unacknowledged – we remove ourselves from the other as far as possible. We play their game: we separate ourselves from them and cut off all contact, as they have done to us. We become the living symbol of their rejection; we think we are in control, but in reality, we have given our power to them.

Ann continues, "Not only did I find perverse ease in physical isolation, cutting myself off from friends, family, comfort and helping hands, but also in the desolate isolation of suicidal fantasies. I made my first attempt at ending it at fourteen, and once even tried cutting my wrists."

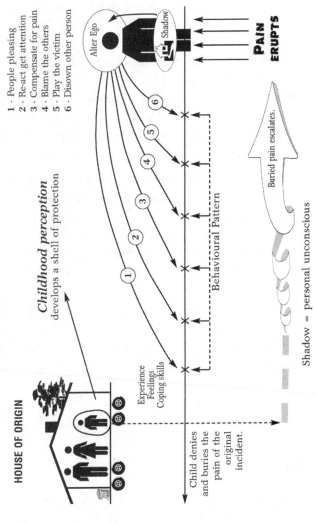

PROGRESSION OF COPING SKILLS.

HOUSE OF ORIGIN

Childhood perception
develops a shell of protection

1 - People pleasing
2 - Re-act get attention
3 - Compensate for pain
4 - Blame the others
5 - Play the victim
6 - Disown other person

Alter Ego

Shadow

PAIN ERUPTS

Behavioural Pattern

Experience
Feelings
Coping skills

Child denies
and buries the
pain of the
original
incident.

Buried pain escalates.

Shadow = personal unconscious

93

When We Become Powerless

I hit bottom. I admit to myself that I am lost and alone. I have rendered myself powerless and helpless. This is step 1 of the 12 Steps.

Jane coped with her pain by secretly eating alone and developed an addiction to cookies. But when her coping skill could no longer deaden the pain, her uncontrollable anger surfaced and her seven-year-old daughter suffered the consequences. Jane's powerlessness over her anger made her ready to seek healing.

> Only when I exhaust all solutions and hit bottom do I begin to turn somewhere, to search for a power greater than myself. This is when our pain and powerlessness become our gift. We realize we can no longer tolerate the agony, we have to reach out for help. We accept that we have to turn it over to God.

Ann, too, eventually became powerless. She says, "Later I became filled with dark urges to fling myself into the path of an oncoming truck. Finally I got scared enough to look for help, never really believing that I could be helped: I was more sinful, more guilty, more crazy than anyone else in the whole wide world. I got so sick of myself. I finally realized that I was powerless."

Sheer Silence

At Bountyfull we do not focus on people's frantic, suicidal feelings. Rather, we help them to relate the incidents that have caused the panic and the suicidal feelings back to the original trauma. This approach relieves the trauma and the fear and helps them focus on concrete situations, which results in a much more rational atmosphere in the session. We follow the story by tracing anger, violence, the threat of self-inflicted pain, or depression to discern the hidden root of the brokenness.

The prophet Elijah tells us in beautiful, poetic language that God is not to be found in the violent winds that shatter our lives and separate us from each other, in the earthquakes within that destroy the foundations of our being, or in the fires of anger that consume us. God is in the sheer silence of peacefulness within our souls.

> [The word of the LORD] said to him....
> "Go out and stand on the mountain before the LORD,
> for the Lord is about to pass by."
> Now there was a great wind, so strong that it was splitting mountains and breaking rocks in pieces before the LORD,
> but the LORD was not in the wind;
> and after the wind an earthquake,
> but the LORD was not in the earthquake;
> and after the earthquake a fire,
> but the LORD was not in the fire;
> and after the fire a sound of sheer silence.
> When Elijah heard it, he wrapped his face in his mantle and went out....
> Then there came a voice to him that said,
> "What are you doing here, Elijah?"
> He answered, "I have been very zealous for the LORD, the God of hosts."
>
> *(1 Kings 19:11-14)*

"Spirit Killers"

We have seen how negative behavioural patterns and addictions take away our freedom to choose life, to nourish our life spirit. How does this happen? Why do so many people unknowingly harbour what I call "spirit killers" within their being and fall into this choice of death or death-dealing ways of living, rather than living life to the full?

At Bountyfull we designate the devastating feelings, such as fear, anger, resentment, guilt and shame, as spirit killers. These feelings become part of that repressed, denied shadow part of our being, the grave that hides all the painful experiences of our forgotten past. Spirit killers may fill a person with fear, anger or rage, or cause depression. We bury not only the pain of the actual incident, but all the surrounding devastating feelings that it caused to emerge.

The repressed pain of the original incident and all the accompanying feelings that have been relegated to the shadow quietly fester and grow throughout the years, and continue to affect and dominate our lives. We are not consciously aware of what lurks within the shadow. Some unrelated incident can unexpectedly trigger and hook that buried feeling, and cause it to erupt in our everyday lives.

Hooked by Our Shadow

How do we allow ourselves to become trapped or hooked by these extremely powerful death-dealing spirit killers? These spirit killers, which live within our hearts, are the negative driving force or motivation that has characterized our deviant behaviours.

The hidden feelings within our shadow can be activated by various incidents or by characteristics of other people, called "hooks." These hooks are like Velcro; from the shadow of our past story they catch all the repressed pain and accompanying feelings of fear, guilt, anger or shame.

"Trudy," who had been married for 35 years, gradually became hooked by her husband's rage.

Trudy's Story: "I Can't Stand up to Him"

Six months before our session, Trudy and her husband decided to take a holiday. She was generally overwhelmed by fear of his rage when she would not submit to his every command. She thought she had gained much strength in relating to him, but as the departure date approached she panicked, collapsed and had to be taken to the hospital. They thought she was having a heart attack. Luckily, it was not a heart attack, but a panic attack. Now, another trip was planned, this time to celebrate their 35th wedding anniversary, and once more she was filled with apprehension. "I can't stand up to him," she told me. "Something will not let me, even though I know he is acting like a raging child. He makes a slave of me and, in fear, I have submitted to his rage all my life."

This image of a "raging child" was like a lightning bolt that carried her back to the memory of herself as a child at her mother's feet, trembling in fear at her mother's rage. In her mother's eyes, Trudy was the "raging child" who needed to be chastized for throwing tantrums. Suddenly Trudy became aware of what had rendered her powerless recently. She realized that she was hooked by her compassion for her husband, because he reminded her of herself as a child. She could not stand up to him because she feared that if she chastized him as a "raging child," she would become her raging mother. In reality, it was the fear of becoming like her mother, and not her fear of her husband's anger, that controlled her and rendered her powerless.

In Trudy's story I sensed the dynamism of the feeling-toned phrase that made her powerless: "I can't stand up to him…something will not let me." That phrase indicated to me that something in her story was much more frightening and powerful than her husband's rage. But it was the phrase "his rage and his anger" that took her back to the original incident with her mother. As a child living in fear of her mother's rage, she vowed that she would never treat anyone else this way.

Finally, Trudy let her mother go, and chose to come back to life instead, back from the land of exile. "What a waste of a lifetime!" she exclaimed. But what a wealth of insight she had gained. She took back her own power and lovingly continued to confront her husband when he was angry. Her 35th wedding anniversary arrived, and she freely accepted her husband's invitation for a month-long vacation down south. Because she now had the strength to "stand up to him" with serenity and peace, it was a great holiday.

Hearts of Stone into Hearts of Flesh

At Bountyfull, our goal and purpose is to support that life-giving beat of the heart that yearns for freedom and life to the full. But handling that heart is difficult; it is so delicate and can so easily be broken again. Isaiah 42 cautions the prophet "not to break the crushed reed or to quench the flickering flame." Our task is to delicately fan that flickering flame back into a fullness of life by the fresh air of what we call the cognitive awareness of how that prison was formed.

A steady stream of pilgrims who have lived their lives in these foreign lands within hearts of stone have passed through Bountyfull's doors, and over them God has poured cleansing water. We have walked patiently and joyfully with countless people returning home within themselves, becoming one with their own being, their ancestors, and their God. In them we sense the beat of a new heart, a spirit revived. Their hearts of stone are replaced by hearts of flesh. They are filled with the joy of the discovery of their true selves. Wherever they walk when they leave our doors, they will fulfill again in their own way God's ancient prophecy: "You will be my people and I will be your God" (Ezekiel 36:28).

5

Grain of Wheat

"Unless a grain of wheat falls into the earth and dies,
it remains just a single grain;
but if it dies, it bears much fruit."

(John 12:24)

Our hope at Bountyfull is to help people break through the shell around their hearts that is both a sanctuary and a prison. That breakthrough is like a birth – the seed bursts forth into life, the chick bursts through the shell of the egg.

Traditional counselling has often tried to change these "problem people," to medicate them or to teach them to correct their dysfunctional behaviours. Some we punish or incarcerate, rather than striving to discover the roots of their pain. In a sense we're asking them to speak our language, when in fact they need to learn to see their dysfunctional behavioural patterns as a foreign language expressed in words and symbolic actions. If only we could comprehend and interpret the language of their pain for them! If only we felt free to enjoy the privilege of discovering the mystery of their lives, rather than becoming overwhelmed or angered by the magnitude of their problems.

Any attempt to break through this shell from the outside by aggressive counselling will reinforce that protective stance they developed as children. The breakthrough can come only from the inside, when people get a glimpse of what has locked them into this shell of their buried pain.

Destructive behaviours and coping skills have the power to set us free when we openly and honestly face them and discern the depth of their meaning – in our present lives, and in the history of our brokenness.

The Hunger to be Released from Pain

That hunger for nourishment reminds me of a parable Jesus told about a man who decided to host a great feast. He invited many people, and sent his slaves to say to those who had been invited, "Everything is ready; come." But the guests would not come.

He said to his slaves, "The wedding is ready,
but those invited were not worthy.
Go therefore into the main streets,
and invite everyone you find to the wedding banquet."
Those slaves went out into the streets and gathered all
whom they found, both good and bad;
so the wedding hall was filled with guests.

(Matthew 22:8-10)

Invited to the wedding feast today are all of us who are in touch with our own broken hearts and yearn to sit at the Master's table. This parable is addressed to all of us who are hungry – not only for food, but for release from the prisons of our own depression and fear. In the parable, those who were originally invited were too preoccupied with the burdens of their own daily living, enjoying the riches and the comforts of their existence, to attend the feast.

Today, not much has changed. We are busy with household chores, caring for the family, working, surfing the Internet, or travelling. We say, "We cannot come."

It is hard to shake people out of the lethargy of pursuing pleasure and wealth until some tragedy, some pain, devastates them and brings them back to their senses. Only then do they begin to see that their source of power and strength has collapsed, because it has been based on material goods.

Today, some who are hungry for wholeness and healing mistakenly try to deaden the pain by drowning it with chemical addictions, or by stuffing it with food, or by escaping from it by developing other destructive behavioural patterns.

In the parable, those invited at the last minute, knowing that they were hungry and hurting, gladly responded to the invitation. The key to successful healing is that kind of hunger. If anyone has been forced to get help, if they're doing it simply to satisfy the requirements of society or to keep the peace in the family, it will not work. At Bountyfull we have committed ourselves to work with anyone who comes to us out of a hunger for healing, freedom or peace within their broken hearts.

Mabel's Story: "A Factory-like Atmosphere"

"Mabel," a gentle, loving mother, had become a compulsive gambler. She felt safe and happy in the casino setting, and was hooked by its mysterious power. Her life had become unmanageable. She had been caught shoplifting, which caused many family problems. Worst of all, she had gambled away all the family's money and now they were deeply in debt. She had jeopardized her marriage and was neglecting her children. To flee from this pain, she gravitated to the casino and gambling. As her problems mounted, she contemplated suicide while crossing the bridge on her way home from the casino one night. This frightened her so much she went to her doctor for help; he, in turn, referred her to me.

I began to probe the effect the atmosphere of the casino had on her, what it meant to her, and why she kept going back there knowing that she would plunge more deeply into despair as a result.

As she told her story, she was suddenly overcome by a feeling she had often had as a child. She referred to "finding sanctuary and safety" when she worked in a "factory-like" atmosphere in her family's shoemaking business at home. As a child in a foreign country, she had frequently been abused by a family member but could not tell anyone. As a coping skill, she found safety in this anonymous factory-like setting where she was surrounded by people who were totally involved in their work, and therefore safe from her predator.

Many years later, when she was introduced to casino gambling, it immediately gave her a comforting, safe feeling. She didn't realize that it was a very close experience to the factory-like setting in her home, where she was totally occupied with her work and safe from interference from any other source. Unconsciously she had recreated the original atmosphere from her childhood experience, which put her in touch with much fear, pain and guilt. To flee from this pain, she returned to the casino and gambling where, in that busy, clamorous atmosphere, she felt safe and comforted. No one was even aware of her presence there, and she did not have to interact with anyone; she was totally occupied with gambling.

The casino's factory-like atmosphere hooked Mabel into her painful past. Unconsciously, she punished herself and fled from her current family, unaware that her pain started in her family of origin.

Mabel's coping skill had become an uncontrollable behaviour pattern and had driven her to despair. As she contemplated suicide while she crossed the bridge over the fast-flowing river on a cold, rainy night, she paused and prayed for help. Just then she was approached by a young man who was lost. He was shivering with cold. She not only comforted him, but gave him her coat and walked with him across the bridge and helped him find his way. With a prayer of thanks to God for saving them both, she returned home.

I recently received a report from her doctor; for the past year and a half since our session, Mabel has been free of her gambling obsession. As a result, the family financial situation has vastly improved, and so has her relationship with her husband.

Mabel realized that her deep yearning for peace and serenity was the gift that brought her to the awareness of the hidden pain within her story. It was this yearning and hunger that ultimately allowed her to break through that protective shell in which her spirit was buried. When she was able to touch that peace and serenity within, she regained her strength and energy and burst through the shell into freedom.

Childhood Perception: "Give up All Your Possessions"

In the healing process, the childhood perception is the key insight that allows the breakthrough to freedom. In the gospel of Luke, Christ says:

> "Whoever comes to me and does not hate father and mother, [spouse] and children, brothers and sisters, yes, and even life itself, cannot be my disciple. Whoever does not carry the cross and follow me cannot be my disciple....
> So therefore, none of you can become my disciple
> if you do not give up all your possessions."
>
> *(Luke 14:26-33)*

Many of us were taught as children to "honour your father and mother," and so we feel we cannot speak openly about the hurt and pain we carry from the past. We may feel much anger for past hurts, but the childhood fear of losing our parents' love is a far greater burden.

We often think of "possessions" as material goods. When Luke's forceful language exhorts us to "hate," or vehemently reject, our mother, father, sister, brother, we might try understanding this as referring to the childhood perception we have carried. Perhaps the possessions in this text relate to the spirit killers within our hearts – those things trapped within our protective shell that render us powerless because we are not consciously aware of them.

We hold onto these "possessions" because they have a mysterious, albeit negative, power that reconnects us with our past. Christ calls our attention to these possessions and asks us to give them up in order to follow him.

As people prepare to relate the "exact nature of their wrongs" in the 5th step of a 12-step program, they hesitate to look back on past transgressions, which may awaken strong feelings of guilt or fear. They may fear that, in some way, they have lost their mother's or father's love because they were punished for their behaviour, which made them feel it was their fault. They may have lived for so long with this feeling that unwittingly they become the victim or the helpless, dependent child. They may develop low self-esteem, put themselves down, and feel unworthy.

Some people spend their lives looking for someone or something outside themselves to lift them out of the morass of these feelings. Alternatively, they may unconsciously strike back at whomever they feel has committed them to this prison. In both cases, they find comfort in living the victim role, because it connects them to the significant other and, at the same time, it frees them of the responsibility of owning their own actions.

Until they become aware of what is buried within their shadow, and release this or break through the walls of the shell of their childhood perception, the significant other remains in control.

In a healing session, we help people discover that the negative feelings retained within their shadow (and perhaps all the buried hatred towards their parents or some significant other) come from their childhood perception. The mysterious power of this insight allows them to say anything they have deeply felt for years against their mother, father, sister or brother because they are now speaking to their own body. It always amazes me to see the change in people when they finally feel free to vent the pent-up anger they have been afraid to express, now that they can do this without harming those they love. They are breaking free from the entrapment of the bonds of childhood and taking possession of their own lives, which allows them to regain that lost love of the parent or significant other.

Once they comprehend that the trauma they endured was witnessed through the eyes of a hurting, fearful child, they have a greater understanding of the burden they have carried through the years. With that awareness, the anger they have carried towards the child they once were dissipates and is transformed into compassion and care. When they see that they did not create their negative behavioural pattern by themselves, that it was not their fault, they can begin to release themselves from the destructive feelings of guilt and shame.

Kim's Story: "Getting down to Study"

For years, "Kim" had lived with depression and loss of life spirit, which was awakened every time she faced her qualifying tests in the field of accounting. Passing these tests was necessary for her to achieve professional standing.

As a child, Kim developed phenomenal mathematical skills; she could compute figures in her head even faster than her grandfather could calculate them on his abacus. She was drawn to a career in accounting and worked as an accountant for a large firm. To advance in her career, she wrote the chartered accountancy exams. She wrote them 11 times, and 11 times she failed, because she could never "get down to study." Probing this frustration in her story took her back to her homeland, where she was separated from her parents and grew up with her sister and brother-in-law in their home. As a young girl she spent a lot of time with her brother-in-law, who remodelled the basement to give her a comfortable living space. She had her own bedroom and bathroom and a little study. When she recalled the basement room, it brought back fearful memories of the evening routine. When the day's work was done, her sister would send Kim downstairs to study. Eventually, she would hear her brother-in-law's footsteps coming down the stairs and be filled with fear, for he had abused her sexually many times. She would run to the bathroom, when she could get there ahead of him, lock herself in, and stay there for hours until she felt it was safe to come out. She realized that this childhood fear was awakened in her every time she was faced with the challenge of getting down to study. Those very words – "getting down to study" – held her spirit captive and locked her within the shell of her powerlessness. Her coping skill, she realized, was to avoid any occasion of getting down to study, which was why she had failed her accounting exams 11 times. This brought about the unbelievable realization that the sexual abuse continued until she was 11 years old, when she moved out of the house and buried her fears. In later years she was often in her brother-in-law's company, but never felt free to speak of those fearful nights in the basement.

On her last visit to Bountyfull, she told me that she finally found the courage to tell her sister what she had lived through, and left it up to her sister to confront her husband. In her own heart, Kim felt free, energized because she had let go of her guilt; she realized that she had taken on not only his guilt, but her sister's as well. When she gave back the guilt, she set herself free and was able to pass the exam.

Kim visited Bountyfull recently to tell us that she now has a very successful career. She feels at ease, no longer feels threatened by any male presence, and is doing exceptionally well.

Breakthrough to Freedom

Once that revelation happens, a realignment unconsciously takes place within the psyche, and their spirit bursts through the protective shell that has numbed the pain. People change right before our very eyes. Suddenly they open up and a weight is lifted from their shoulders; they sense once more the life-giving energy within their hearts. They reconnect with their own spirit, become alive and wake up. Old relationships and connections that have controlled and taken away freedom are almost instantly dissolved in that awareness. They become more mature and conscious, regain their sense of being present to themselves, and discover that the answers to freedom lie within.

The healing that takes place in the story of a person's pain and brokenness is not unlike the mystery of the grain of wheat that has to fall into the ground and die to break through the shell of imprisonment before it can come to life. Healing is truly a breakthrough that happens when people become cognitively aware of the root of the problem, and consciously identify the significant others who were the cause. They name them, claim them, let them go, and break through to freedom with a new energy, a new sense of hope. They come to life.

After a session at Bountyfull, we do not book regular appointments in advance, expecting that people will continue to need our help. I do not encourage the client to become dependent upon me, the counsellor. Once their broken spirit has been awakened and they have rediscovered the treasure of their true self, I encourage them to own their new insight, live with that new awareness, and feel free to call again if they feel the need.

6

Treasure in a Field

"The kingdom of heaven is like treasure hidden in a field,
which someone found and hid; then in his joy
he goes and sells all that he has and buys that field."
(Matthew 13:44)

Human beings have a unique gift: we can reflect on our history and probe within the depths of our own being. This allows us to discover how we operate, what goes on within us, and what gives us life.

At Bountyfull we see the gospel parable quoted above as a guideline for our reflection on our life story, and see the field as a symbol of that story. Our goal is to help people find a sense of hope as they dig into the earthiness of their being, into the buried hurts of their past and discover there the treasure that is their true self. All of us must "own" our whole story, and not run away from it or deny it. Like the man in the gospel who bought the field, we not only review and examine our life story, we are challenged to accept it in its totality. In the parable, not only the buried treasure but the whole field becomes his possession; he owns it. This allows him to dig freely in that field to find the hidden treasure again. We, too, must name and claim our story to unearth the treasure of our true selves.

Nothing is as mysterious and as complicated as our human psyche, which is an integral part of our being. Instead of feeling overwhelmed by the phenomenal task before us, we must learn to open wide our eyes in amazement and wonder at the great God-given gift of life and focus on the gift of our unique life spirit.

Seeing Life as a Story

At Bountyfull we help people see their life as a story, rather than simply focusing on the litany of their wrongdoings and dysfunctional behaviours. For us, life is not just a linear succession of events; life is a story, and life stories are the tales of broken hearts. Our stories are the unfolding of the mystery of our personal lives, encompassing both good and bad. The words and behavioural patterns we use are tools for survival. In cases of dysfunction, they can be threatening, angry or destructive. This dynamic becomes evident as we trace a life story. People we accompany come to the awareness that their behavioural patterns convey a message to others, while at the same time alleviating their own pain.

At Bountyfull we do not attempt to change behavioural patterns by trying to make people conform to the demands of society. We go beyond the problems to the fascinating world of the messages hidden in the dynamic phraseology they use, or the bizarre messages of their dysfunctional behavioural patterns. The unique phraseology reveals how they have survived intolerable pain. The key is to realize that the phraseology and the behavioural patterns are attempts to compensate for the buried pain.

A Journey of Discovery

With our clients, we journey along the path of pain and trauma, knowing that behavioural patterns, like weeds, have almost overgrown the path to hide the traces of the painful journey.

We begin a journey of discovery with each new person who comes to us for healing. As we have seen in the previous stories, this is a journey to freedom. It is achieved by digging into the painful incidents of the past to unearth the treasure of their lost sense of self that is buried in their shadow, their unconscious.

Our task as we accompany them is to be open to the mystery of the broken heart that unfolds before us. It is the very gift of people's pain that opens up the graves in which their hearts have been entombed. Buried in their memories lies a wealth of experience that has been denied and forgotten. We can help them rediscover this wealth if we create the proper atmosphere as we delicately begin to probe the shadow of repressed memories.

Each story contains hurts people have learned to hide or deny. The task is to walk these pathways again, but this time, without fear and with trust, peace and confidence. They must feel and acknowledge their pain, must own it and embrace it, in order to take the fear out of it. We must never take away the gift of the anguish of that personal discovery of self.

The challenge for us is to strive to allow people to discover for themselves how to break through the protective shell they have constructed and let that imprisoned life spirit move freely. They have but to awaken that energizing gift of the life power that is buried within, and choose life. We help them develop the skills to discover that treasure of the self, to dig within their life story to find it. This treasure is the "kingdom," the spirit of God within, that all of us seek.

As we saw in Chapter 5, we do not begin to make an in-depth search into our life story until we have been reduced to powerlessness or helplessness. We can achieve true healing only when we have acknowledged our powerlessness. Only then do we develop a hunger and a willingness to search within and to turn our lives over to some power greater than ourselves. With that awareness, our brokenness can become our gift.

Following and Charting the Life Story

Following the life story involves learning how to hear and interpret each person's unique language. People are like the book that tells the hidden story of their lives.

The task is to grasp the mystery of that story without trying to solve the problems that are presented. What is it that stirs the bushes of past memories, ruffles the leaves, or lights up the foliage with flashes of radiant bursts of sunlight? We learn to cherish these clues and pause to discover the source of the movement. Problems must be viewed with care and understanding, of course, but kept in perspective with the life story.

What touches and moves the body? As we read the story in their eyes, we must also learn to read the body language. What do the body movements, the posture, the tears, the smiles convey? The body carries the story of the years. It bears the scars and knows the pain, because it has been used to hide the deeper pain that is buried in the psyche. It is important to be keenly attuned to any bodily messages that can be observed. These may be defensive messages used to protect a sense of self, or aggressive and violent messages to others.

Many things have touched people in their stories, but they are buried in the darkness of the paths that we have feared to walk alone. Our challenge is to follow the clues along the trail of their broken hearts as they tell their story. We must not be disturbed or shocked with whatever darts out of the darkness of denial. We remain calm and caring, no matter what the pain may be. As in Rose's story, pain cannot forever be hidden or denied, no matter how deeply it is buried. We must pick up on the dynamism, the energy of those feeling-toned phrases, that guides us to the hidden pain.

These buried, painful memories affect the body, which offers new insights. We follow in great detail, and with extreme attentiveness, all the messages that the body puts out that reveal the pain that has imprisoned their bodies. We begin to dig in the field of their life story by opening up these painful experiences.

Following a life story becomes a very life-giving experience for me because it demands that I be attentive to all the clues that a person gives me. I watch for the dynamism of the words, which either negatively or positively affect the body or the soma. It is almost like reading a mystery novel, with the story unfolding and leading back to the root of the problem.

Attempting to discover the message of buried pain can be a rich but mysterious experience, as Lucy's story shows.

Lucy's Story: "The Missing Link"

"Lucy" was living on the streets, totally dissociated from her very proper and affluent family. Lucy's mother, who was distraught about this situation, brought her to Bountyfull in the hope that we could help bring her daughter back home. Lucy's parents could not understand why she chose to live on the streets, and saw it as a total rejection of the family and their values.

When I met Lucy, she told me that when she was a little girl, her mother treated her as though she didn't fit into the family. She was not considered important in the family plans, while her brothers received much attention.

Feeling rejected and unimportant, Lucy left home for life on the streets. She became involved in drugs and sex, just like so many other young people on the street do. She felt at home with, and accepted by, these other broken and rejected people.

In recounting her story, Lucy used this throwaway phrase: "I am the missing link in the family, but they do not see me. Without me, the family is not complete. I'm the link that gives it meaning." I asked her to tell me what the word "link" meant to her. She said, "It's like a ring or a single link in a chain." At that point, she became conscious of the ring she was wearing in her eyebrow, which to her was like a link from a chain. It was startling for her to realize that she had chosen to wear the ring right over her eye, not simply to be cool, but to symbolize for herself and for others that "they don't see me." The ring was a symbol of herself, the missing link in the family.

In the course of her session, as Lucy unearthed her buried feelings, she became consciously aware that her lifestyle on the streets was an unspoken message of anger to her parents, particularly her mother. She was acting out in symbol and behavioural pattern what she could not say in words.

Once she became aware of the message of her symbol, she owned her own feelings, reclaimed her life spirit, and freed herself from the control of her mother, who was the significant other in her story. She no longer felt compelled to symbolically act out the feelings she had repressed in her shadow.

Lucy was then capable of addressing the issue directly with her mother and telling her how she really felt. Her mother understood what had caused the rebellious behaviour; she also realized that she missed Lucy and wanted her back as part of the family.

Discerning the Symbols in Our Life Story

In the charting process, the deep, hidden messages that come from the pain of buried hurts are not easily discernible because they can be expressed in a distorted manner – through dysfunctional behavioural patterns and symbols that characterize our life story, as we saw in Lucy's story. These behavioural expressions and symbols are the signposts that guide us back to the forgotten past, which holds the treasure and the mystery of our true self.

The unconscious and spontaneous creation of the meaningful symbols we use in our lives are signs of a spirit yearning to be free of the repressed relationships within the shadow of our inner selves.

These numinous relationships and mystifying symbols, which express the buried pain in the unconscious, are the main focus of our listening process at Bountyfull. Symbols, which are a bridge between the unconscious and the conscious, are much more tangible than the feeling-toned phrases. For me, the beauty of symbols is that they are one level above the intangible compensatory relationships. In their own unique way, symbols give expression to these relationships.

In a mysterious way, our stories symbolize our historical relationship with our inner selves. A symbol, which can be the mythic story of our lives, is not to be looked *at*, but looked *through*. It allows us to peer into the depths of our human experience and discover the hidden messages for the healing of our broken hearts (John Shea, *Stories of God*, p. 66).

As we have seen, our broken hearts yearn for freedom and healing, and yet continually send messages that may contradict that yearning. As you will recall from Jane's story in Chapter 4, Dad's Cookies were the symbol that held the hidden messages of her repressed pain and her yearning to reconnect with her father and to be freed from the guilt of his abuse. Her symbol was the key that unlocked the pain buried within her.

People become powerless when they unconsciously give over their freedom and rational behaviour and are driven by these symbols. Our challenge is to learn to see through the symbols to the messages being conveyed. In this way, dysfunctional behavioural patterns become the key to release us from the slavery of our early childhood perceptions.

In Kim's story (see Chapter 5), the constant frustration expressed in her symbol and her dynamic phrase "I can't get down to study" reveals the pain of her sense of powerlessness as well as her yearning to free herself from entrapment. Pain evokes these messages and symbols, which are the compensatory relationships we strive to discover, the spiritual connections that reveal our broken hearts. They encompass the pain of brokenness, the struggle to be free, and the direction we must take to attain freedom. These relationships are the very avenues that guide us in the discovery of the hidden pain and indicate what must be faced or overcome to facilitate the healing process.

The symbols are as unique as a signature to every story and are often found in the familiar phrases that we unconsciously repeat, or in the symbols that become the vehicles of expression of our life story.

As we begin to discover the root of the problem, we must discern the unconscious symbol that has defined the life story, and see how that symbol has become the script for the story. That awareness can bring a spiritual awakening, revealing the source of the compulsion or pain.

You will recall that Kim was addicted to failure and bouts of depression. Without thinking, she continually referred to the 11 times she had failed her chartered accountancy exams and used the phrase "I just can't get down to study." Simple phrases like that one carry many messages that indicate available avenues for healing if we search deeply. Even the careless, offhand or angry use of some favourite phrase supplies a great deal of information about the source of the pain, how we originally suffered it, and how, even as adults, we remain trapped. Our broken heart, in its yearning for peace, freedom and justice, wreaks a path of destruction for others and, ultimately, for us.

A Psychological Block: A Protective Wall

As we begin each session, people have the opportunity to name and claim their feelings around their present trauma. We search with probing questions, such as "When did this happen?" "Did you ever feel this way before?" "What was the situation?" "Where did this begin?" Often people say they cannot remember: this is a psychological block.

I see the block as a protective wall that their psyche has developed to allow them to hide within the repressed area of pain rather than face it and open it up. I don't stop or focus on the block, because that would bring the whole process to a halt. If I allow them to focus on the block, they are not free to touch the hidden pain because their intellect has taken over.

To get beyond the block to the source of the pain, I challenge the person to recall concrete experiences, or to contextualize that pain in their story. When they recreate or recall a concrete experience, they are unconsciously carried beyond the block.

By posing these probing questions, I distract the person from the block and continue to chart their story as they relate it.

I ask questions to recreate the situation, the location, the time of day, who was present, and what they felt at that time. They then begin to formulate the surrounding ambience of where the incident took place. It is like recreating the total atmosphere, including the physical characteristics of the room, what was happening, who was present and how it affected them. Without challenging the block, we have subtly moved beyond it, allowing them to open up previously repressed memories. Unconsciously they also become intrigued, if not enthralled, with the story as it unfolds. They may even marvel at the child they were in the situation, and how clever the child was to be able to survive and develop protective coping skills that provided a sense of safety in the midst of the trauma. They name and claim the feelings they had in a concrete situation.

Jane's Story: "A Pinprick of Light"

In Chapter 4 we met Jane, whose dysfunction was overeating. In this session we had to delve a little deeper, because she was experiencing a block that would not permit her to come in touch with the roots of the pain, which were the feelings of guilt and shame hidden behind the block. These repressed feelings filled her with a fear that would overwhelm her almost daily in a variety of situations, especially with her husband. Jane told me that one morning when she went to work, she was very upset and anxious about a situation at home. Let's listen to the story in her own words.

> My husband frequently asks me to type documents for him in his office, which is in the basement of our home. Last evening, he insisted that I do the task immediately, saying it would take only five minutes. I soon realized that the job would require much more of my time than I could give. The children were upstairs unattended. I was very anxious about this and wanted to leave, but my husband became angry and insisted that I stay to finish the typing. I felt very angry, shaky and afraid. I shouted at my husband and started to cry, but then I stayed to finish the job anyway.

In the session, Larry asked me to tell him about feeling anxious. It was difficult to attach being anxious to any one thing in particular; it was such a regular part of my day.

Jane: When I'm anxious, I can't think clearly. I get mixed up, can't concentrate.

Larry: So what do you do?

Jane: Sometimes I forget even what I'm doing or where I am; everything goes blank and I start to float away, up over my right shoulder.

Larry: When this happens, where are you?

Jane: It's very confusing. I don't remember anything at all.

Larry: What do you see?

Jane: It's weird, just a pinprick of light.

Larry: A pinprick of light, where?

Jane: Coming through the green blind.

Larry: Where is the green blind?

Jane: I feel sick in the pit of my stomach and it hurts. The lump in my throat hurts so much, too. I cry so hard and I don't even know why. There's nothing in my head. I can't think of anything, I don't remember anything. My heart is racing so fast it feels like it will explode.

Larry asks the questions slowly, waiting for the answer.

Larry: Where are you? Is it day or night? Who is there? How old are you?

Jane: I remember, but I really don't want to.

It's Mom and Dad's bedroom. It is sunny outside and there are pinpricks of light coming through the green blind pulled over the window. Dad comes home from work and I'm really glad that I don't have to have a nap alone. I love him and he gives me lots of attention. It feels so nice and cozy to be with him.

Something changes and I feel bad and sad and mad. I have to be very quiet so Mom doesn't hear. I want Dad to love me, but I didn't want this. I shouldn't be here, I should be somewhere else. If I tell him, he'll be mad at me, he won't love me. I'm afraid.

I float up and away, there's a bright little crack of light coming through the green blind. It's all blank. I don't think about anything, just the bright, bright light. It's a really important place, that little light. I won't forget it. It's so bright, I stare at it for a long time; it feels like years. I don't see anything or feel anything else.

Suddenly, the light is gone and Mom is there. She picks me up and is angry. Dad is angry. They are angry at me. I should have been quiet. I'm sorry. No one hears me now. I feel sick in the pit of my stomach. Go away, they say. Mom cries. No one looks at me. No one sees me. I am five. I'm bad, wrong. I am all alone. It's all my fault. I am sorry.

Jane continues,

In the session, my heart is pounding so hard and fast it feels like I could die. I can't breathe. I want it to stop. In my panic, I was aware that Larry was calm, and he quietly asked me a question which brought me back to the present, and removed the childhood fear that had gripped my heart. With one simple question, I was an adult once more recalling the recent situation in the basement at the computer with my husband. I had faced it and survived.

My heart slows down but I still feel anxious. This typing job was only supposed to take five minutes. I can't do this, it's more time than I have to give. I feel afraid, I know he's going to get mad. I can feel myself floating up and away, over my right shoulder. I can't think clearly. I get angry, swearing and yelling at my husband. We have a huge fight. How could he make me do this, with the kids upstairs alone? I shouldn't be here, I should be somewhere else. I stay at the computer working anyway. My husband is very angry and tells me to get out. He won't talk to me or look at me. I go upstairs to the children, but I'm not even really there. I just putter around, crying, angry, afraid. I feel so guilty because I should be downstairs helping him. I'm so angry because he asks more of me than I can give and I'm afraid he won't love me anymore.

This type of scenario, with some variation, occurred repeatedly in our marriage relationship. For so long, I felt hopeless about the situation, very depressed and quite helpless to do anything about it. Now I can see that when present-day circumstances bring up buried feelings that hook me into the past, I go right back to my childhood coping skill. I go blank, float away – like I did into that pinprick of light. I become enraged at the feeling of guilt I carry for something that was not my fault. Those childhood feelings of fear and guilt, hidden away and accelerating in the darkness of my shadow for so many years, killed my spirit, my sense of self.

When my husband wanted me to help him with his work, I wanted to please him because I was fearful that he wouldn't "love" me. At the same time, leaving the children alone upstairs didn't feel "right." All this fear and guilt hooked me into my buried childhood feelings and I was reduced to acting like a frightened child. Overwhelmed, and "invaded" with this negative energy, I was "beside myself" with emotion and not free to respond as an adult woman.

Through the session and charting, following my own story and phrases, I saw how those familiar feelings kept Mom and Dad close to me. I realized later that that was the negative payoff. Strangely enough, every time I entertain those negative feelings, I unconsciously go back to my association with Mom and Dad when I was just a child. I became aware that my negative feelings were a means of holding onto my mom and dad; they kept me in my childhood and brought me the "comfort" of being in the company of my parents. This realization allowed me to let my parents go by accepting the past and giving them back their own feelings of fear and guilt that I had been carrying since childhood. I became free and I reclaimed my sense of self.

Serenity: "Acceptance, Courage and Wisdom"

As Jane told her story, it was clear that she was facing a very difficult and traumatic situation. At Bountyfull we do not walk alone. We walk in the prayerful presence of God's continual guidance and healing power. I handle a critical situation, such as Jane's, with the awareness of God's healing spirit in her as well as in me. As I walked through her painful journey with her, in my mind I quietly placed her in the presence of God, which allowed me to remain focused, to avoid getting caught in her panic and fear.

I guided her through the healing process by helping her to personalize the Serenity Prayer for herself. It is that personal acceptance of the fact of the past as past, and the positive direction of taking back our lives and facing the future with confidence and freedom, that brings healing.

In summary form, in her own words, Jane concluded:

God grant me the serenity to accept the things I cannot change

"My past: I see it, hold it and accept that I cannot change it."

the courage to change the things I can

"I let go of my childhood perception of guilt and fear;

I am free to own my feelings and respond to others as an adult."

and the wisdom to know the difference

"I have a much greater awareness of the whole picture from the insights I have gained. I open out to the future with trust."

Bill's Story:
"No One Will Cross My Family Again"

> Jesus came to the tomb…he cried with a loud voice,
> "Lazarus, come out!" The dead man came out, his hands and feet bound with strips of cloth, and his face wrapped in a cloth.
> Jesus said to them, "Unbind him, and let him go."
>
> *(John 11:38-44)*

"Bill," a large man in excellent health, was facing multiple charges for repeated, excessive violence and had been charged with bodily assault with intent to commit harm. He had periodically served time in jail, where he had been treated by the psychiatric department in an attempt to change his violent behavioural patterns. He was accompanied by security guards to these appointments as he was considered a violent offender. Because he was not able to overcome these outbursts, he was considered a threat to society and was to be forced to change his behaviour.

In traditional counselling, the counsellor's task would be to help Bill develop affirmative behavioural patterns or, failing that, to refer him to a doctor for the appropriate medication to control his violent outbursts. If neither of these solutions were successful, he would be incarcerated again. By the time Bill was referred to me by his lawyer, he had already served 18 prison terms and was now facing another court case. His lawyer hoped that we might be able to discover the hidden cause of this uncontrollable compulsion.

As we began Bill's session, he was very ill at ease. He told me that others were afraid of him, and he recounted the long history of his violent behaviour. I did not react to these messages or to his aggressive behaviour; I knew he needed to shift the focus from the negativity and the hopelessness of his story in order to understand what had caused the behaviour and whether he had any hope of recovery. To that end, I asked his permission to trace his story on a timeline to give him a clear picture of the number of times he had been jailed and to help him understand what had caused the violent outbursts. I assured him that I had no intention of judging or changing his behaviour. My concern was to help him understand himself better and find the freedom to face his whole life story.

Assuring him that my primary purpose was not to change his behavioural patterns immediately put Bill at ease. I then asked him to look at his life story with understanding and compassion for himself as a child who had endured many painful experiences. He began to describe the difficulties that he had lived through during childhood, hopeful that he could discern the hidden cause of the compulsion that was driving him to violence. He was earnestly seeking to be released from this prison of pain and further incarceration.

Let's chart Bill's journey back to the roots of his childhood trauma. Stay aware of the timeline as we trace the source of his dysfunctional behaviours back to the root of his hidden pain. We will follow the traumatic incidents that are always accompanied by the same dominant feelings.

As we began to trace his story, he told me he was the eldest of three children in an abusive alcoholic family. His mother gave him the responsibility of caring for his two younger sisters. As we tried to discern the root of his anger, he returned to a day when he was a little boy caring for his infant sister, who was in a crib in his room. He became frightened when he saw that she had caught her neck in the slats of the crib and was beginning to strangle. He was terrified and powerless. He tried to alert his parents, but they were drunk and could not respond. By the time they did, his baby sister had died. He buried that terrible pain of her death and his overwhelming sense of powerlessness deep within his heart, along with his anger towards his parents. He vowed then and there that he would personally take care of the family himself.

One day several years later, Bill was coming home from school with his other little sister, who was just five years old. He loved her dearly and had the responsibility of caring for her and bringing her home for lunch each day. As they approached their home, she asked if she could go across the street to her friend's house for lunch, and he agreed. As Bill opened the door into his own house, he heard a motorcycle and the squeal of brakes, and then heard the impact as his sister was struck and killed. Once more he felt completely powerless, helpless and overwhelmed with grief, pain and guilt.

For the first time since the accident, he suddenly remembered that after it happened, he went into the silence of his own room, sat at the edge of his bed, held his head in his hands and made a pact with his little sisters. In his land of exile, in his hopelessness and pain, he created his own language of survival: "No one would ever cross his family again."

I drew a simple timeline from the present back as far as his memory could carry him to his own home and his family of origin. I charted all the incidents he could recall, placing them on the timeline so he could see them in relation to the total picture. As we got back to his childhood, I sketched not only the family members (using stick figures), but also their home. As the diagram below shows, I indicated the trauma he experienced by drawing a shell around the little figure of Bill as a child. This is the shell of denial that was described in previous chapters. Within that shell, I depicted how he had buried the feelings and the pain by indicating that they were trapped within. In order to express how those buried feelings unconsciously pervaded his whole life, I showed how they were repressed in his memory by drawing them beneath the timeline. As his story progressed, that association with the original pain was lost and he allowed the repressed feelings to accelerate to an uncontrollable emotion. He was not conscious that the feelings he'd experienced as a child became charged with more pain, anguish and anger as his story unfolded, eventually turning into uncontrollable rage.

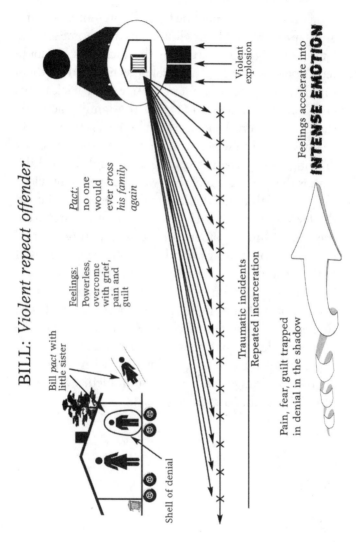

BILL: *Violent repeat offender*

Bill *pact* with little sister

Shell of denial

Feelings:
Powerless, overcome with grief, pain and guilt

Pact:
no one would ever cross his family again

Violent explosion

Traumatic incidents
Repeated incarceration

Pain, fear, guilt trapped in denial in the shadow

Feelings accelerate into
INTENSE EMOTION

Bill understood that the powerless, helpless feelings of childhood had accelerated into the intense emotions buried within his shadow. These emotions were so sensitive, so explosive, they could be triggered without his awareness or control.

As the session continued, he was astounded to find that 17 of his previous 18 charges were related to traffic incidents. Suddenly he realized that in every one of these cases, someone was "crossing" in front of him and endangering the people (especially young children) with him. In every instance, he erupted in uncontrollable, violent rage.

A person's life story can become a succession of these survival techniques or coping skills that help them escape the original pain. They may be compulsive reactions, such as drug addiction, alcohol, gambling or violence, or they may be coping skills that deny the pain and give the impression that the person "has it all together." These skills enable us to run from the pain of rejection, abuse or violence, and are unique to our own life story. They become vehicles of expression in our lives and we become controlled by them.

With the one incident not related to traffic situations, Bill was in a pub with a group of men who began to "playfully rough him up." One man put a stranglehold around his neck. Something snapped inside of Bill, and he beat the man mercilessly without knowing why, ending up in jail once more. In our session, he saw for the first time that this feeling of being strangled awakened that terrifying fear he experienced as a boy when his little sister's head was caught in the slats of her crib.

Bill realized that his uncontrollable rage erupted from the hidden pain and the grief, loss and guilt he had carried all his life. The violent rage was the expression of the buried pain that he thought could never be healed. His only release from the guilt was his uncontrollable violence. He had buried himself in that dark prison within, which protected him from that early pain, but also sent a very strong message to everyone else.

His violent behaviour became the survival technique by which he denied or buried the original trauma. The dysfunctional behavioural patterns became all-consuming addictions that trampled the clues on the pathway back to the original hurt. Unconsciously, Bill became trapped in his compulsions and was unable to free himself.

Like Bill, many people can become blindsided by the force of a current experience that, in an instant, can transport them back through the years to a buried hurt from childhood. Once that pain is touched, it can unconsciously activate the accumulated anguish of the years and cause the person to explode in a violent reaction; they become "bound" and live within the prisons of their own creation.

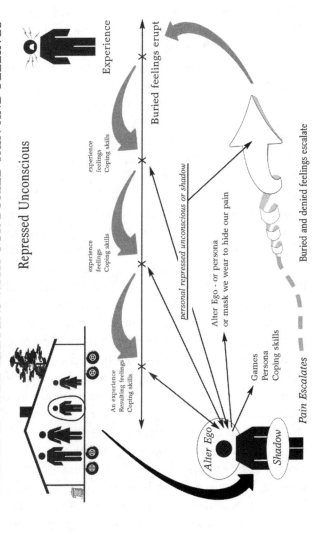

DIAGRAM OF WHAT HAPPENS WITH OUR BURIED PAIN AND FEELINGS

Repressed Unconscious

Experience

Buried feelings erupt

experience
feelings
Coping skills

experience
feelings
Coping skills

An experience
Resulting feelings
Coping skills

personal repressed unconscious or shadow

Alter Ego - or persona
or mask we wear to hide our pain

Games
Persona
Coping skills

Buried and denied feelings escalate

Alter Ego

Shadow

Pain Escalates

Bill was amazed to see how the symbol of that pact he made with his little sisters had literally put him in prison all these years and kept him in prison within his own broken heart. The awareness of the symbol of that pact burst the shell of denial and allowed him to rediscover his lost sense of self. In turn he made peace with both his sisters because, to the best of his ability, he had lived up to his responsibility for them. This released him from his sense of guilt.

He saw that none of this pain would have happened in his own life or in the lives of his sisters if his parents had been loving and responsible people. Their deviant alcoholic behaviour had devastated his early childhood years; he had denied that anger and buried it deep within him. He could not get past his own overwhelming guilt. During our session, he acknowledged that as a child he was not guilty; rather, it was the adults who had not lived up to their responsibility. Unwittingly, children take on guilt for a tragedy because in their minds, adults are always right, so they themselves must be at fault. Bill realized that all these years he had carried his parents' guilt. He was now able to give back the guilt to his parents, rather than carrying it himself. Unconsciously he had been trying to change the past, to eradicate that guilt, by taking out his anger on innocent victims rather than acknowledging that the root of his anger was his own parents. He had to face that anger towards them, place the blame back on their shoulders and thus set himself free. He did not have to solve the problem, because it was never his in the first place. That full understanding of where the real root of the problem lay freed him from the tomb of his imprisonment.

As we charted his story, Bill uncovered the mystery of his childhood perception and the surrounding feelings, and saw that those feelings were the root of his present problems. Until that moment he had never been able to face that pain because it was an intolerable memory to resurrect. That childhood perception, and all the pain around it, developed into the destructive behavioural pattern that became more sophisticated with each incident.

Our concern at Bountyfull is to heal the broken heart and to help people find the freedom and the energy to mend their dysfunctional behaviour. Uncontrollable addictions to alcohol, drugs or violent behaviour are a form of self-medication to numb the pain. Bill's dysfunctional behaviours came from the intolerable pain of a broken heart. When he could comprehend this, he was able to overcome the stigma and the fear of discovering the exact nature of his wrongs (step 4 of the 12 Steps).

Once Bill had a cognitive awareness of how he formed that protective shell, his spirit was reawakened. He discovered that his childlike coping skills were in fact an extremely clever means of survival that helped to take the pain out of the discovery of the brokenness in his life, and allowed him to appreciate himself as a child.

In our session, as he unravelled each thread of the web of guilt and anger in which he was entangled, he gradually became unbound and set himself free. In the healing, by relating the Serenity Prayer to his life story, he openly addressed his mother, his father and his two sisters. With a new-found energy, he let his mother and his father go free; he released his own body, broke through the shell and came out of the tomb of his imprisonment. He accepted the past with clarity and insight. Bill discovered in his story that the "kingdom" is actually a place within himself, where he found the life-giving spirit of a loving God. Now, as a mature person, he was enabled to enter into that pain and, with his belief in God, to walk through it to freedom.

In the eyes of the court, Bill was an incorrigible violent offender. He was a "hopeless case," a repeat offender, bound by his uncontrollable rage. And yet, as we saw in his story, he was able to free himself and to find hope for the future.

Now that he knows the source of the problem, he has to keep it in mind, to own his anger while it remains related to the incident that caused it, and to prevent it from accelerating again. I explained to him that when he is aware of a feeling, he can own it and deal with it; but if he does not deal with it and continues to bury it as he did before, that accumulated pent-up feeling of anger will become rage, and then the emotion "has him."

Presently Bill is not only out of jail, but sharing a happy relationship with a close friend and her daughter. Not long ago, on Boxing Day, I stopped by Bountyfull to do some cleaning up and saw Bill and his little family at the door. He had driven in from out of town to say thanks and to leave a generous donation. Their visit added a lot to the Christmas message of "Peace on earth."

All of the stories in this book reveal in unique and personal ways how people are filled with a craving far beyond that of the chemical addictions to which they are enslaved or the behavioural pattern that is destroying their lives. Each story speaks unmistakably of that deeply buried God-given gift of God's spirit that is always alive within us, no matter how much we ignore it or choose destruction over a life of love, unity, peace and fulfillment.

7

Interpersonal Relationships

"How can you say to your neighbour, 'Friend, let me take out the speck in your eye,' when you yourself do not see the log in your own eye? You hypocrite, first take the log out of your own eye, and then you will see clearly to take the speck out of your neighbour's eye...."

(Luke 6:42)

Holy Ground

In looking at interpersonal relationships and marital problems, we examine conflicts in their proper perspective, and once more make this a journey of discovery. Here we are entering a sacred place, the holy ground within our beings, where we hold most dear those we cherish. In order to touch that sacred place, we have to be honest enough to hold up the mirror to ourselves and to begin to discover, with freedom and joy, what upsets us in our relationships with others, especially in the intimate relationships within marriage and families. It is a gift for each of us to become aware of what goes on in our own hearts when we have so cleverly and carefully denied our feelings by putting on the mask of our socially acceptable self.

In the Scripture passage quoted above, Christ grabs our attention by using an unusual image. It would be easy to discount this teaching as a pious exaggeration; on closer examination, however, it is a marvellous symbol of the very complicated psychological processes of judging, blaming and projection. The text reminds us that it is easier to criticize someone else and to blame them for their dysfunctional behaviours than to honestly admit our own failings. Most of us are not aware that we are caught up in this dynamic of judging and blaming. And yet it is these almost imperceptible psychological realities that are the root of the breakdown of many marriages and other relationships.

When I work with people having marital or family problems, my approach is similar to the one I use with the people whose stories I shared earlier in this book: I begin by searching for the root of the problem. The process is more difficult, however, when I deal with more than one person, and especially with more than one generation or with different cultures.

People often come to Bountyfull for counselling because of some problem with their children. As they discover the root of the family problem, they see that their children's problems have dredged up their own buried hurts and fears from childhood. The children are the mirrors of their hidden past. Clients will exclaim, "I came because of a problem with my daughter, and I discovered my own shortcomings!" Only when they contact their own feelings can they deal in a mature way with their children's problems.

Let's listen to Karla's story.

Karla's Story: "I Have to Do Something"

"Karla" came to her first session very upset about her 37-year-old daughter, "Judy." Judy, who had moved out of the house and was living in her own apartment, was abusing drugs and alcohol. During our session, Karla was concerned about leaving in time to meet her younger daughter, "Paula," so they could talk about their next course of action regarding Judy.

Karla related a variety of difficult incidents involving Judy over the years. Judy had upset the whole family, and Karla's husband, who was at his wits' end, had finally said, "That's it. This is the last time we're going to help her." But Karla felt responsible for her daughter, even though Judy was now an adult. Karla wanted to know how much control she had over her daughter and what her role was as a parent. She had always felt she had a lot of control over Judy, but as we talked she realized that Judy had been making her own decisions for some time. At this, Karla felt relieved, as though a burden of guilt had been removed from her shoulders. She seemed to have come to a peaceful solution, and left feeling satisfied with her session.

A few weeks later, Karla phoned me very upset and panicky because she believed Judy was using drugs again. Karla wanted to know what her next move as a parent should be. Because Paula lived right across the street from Judy, Karla had asked Paula to keep an eye on her older sister, to make sure she wasn't acting out again. Paula had just phoned to say she had noticed smoke coming out of the top window of Judy's house, indicating that "they were doing drugs again." Karla felt she had to "do something" about the situation.

In pursuing her feelings, Karla said she felt powerless, didn't know where to turn, and had to seek help to fix the situation. When we talked about her fear and helplessness, she was reminded of a situation in her own home when she was a child. Her older sister had broken the good Christian family rules and had become pregnant in her teens. This devastated Karla's mother; Karla recalls being in the kitchen when her mother exploded and chastized her older sister for getting pregnant. The sister had ruined the family reputation; because of her, everybody would know that her mother was not a good parent.

Karla, filled with fear at her mother's outburst, cowered in the corner because she felt helpless. Desperately she looked for someone else to bring peace to the situation, but there was no one. Her father, an exemplary Christian, was timid and weak – like a "big teddy bear." She could not turn to him or rely on him. From that moment, she promised herself not to let this happen again in her life. Even at a young age, she would take control and assume her father's responsible role in his absence. This childhood survival technique or coping skill seemed to quell her fear and powerlessness.

When Karla got in touch with the dynamics of her early childhood relationship with her mother, her older sister, and her father, and when she recognized the impressions that this dynamic left on her, she had a breakthrough: the present situation was strikingly similar. When Paula phoned to say that her sister was using drugs again, Karla feared that, like her mother, she was not a proper parent because she had not raised her daughter according to Christian principles. She once again became the fearful child cowering in the kitchen. In panic, she looked for someone else to "back her up" and make her feel safe.

As a helpless child, she had given her mother control over her own emotions. She had coped by assuring herself that she would never fall into a similar situation, but she had done just that.

Now she released the power her mother had over her and knew that it was her mother's fear, not her own. She let go of her childhood role of taking over the position of her "teddy bear" father.

Karla had thought she was in control of the family and her daughter. Now she admitted that a mother is not responsible for her 37-year-old daughter's actions. Judy's actions were her own responsibility and there was no way that Karla, as a mother, could change her. Of course, Karla, like any mother, would be greatly disturbed to find out that her daughter was using drugs, but she could not help Judy solve this problem as long as she was hooked by the anger of her own childhood situation. She set Judy free to live her own life while offering to be a loving resource for her.

"Hooked" by Our Children

One of the most common and unexpected sources of hooks in families are the children, who can trigger hidden thoughts or feelings about our own life story. Perhaps we invest our children with all the hopes and dreams we could never accomplish but remain buried within our shadow; or perhaps we think they reflect the kind of parent we are.

Children are a gift from God. Even as infants, they are a message of a whole new creation in their own individuality and personality, a unique gift to our world. It is easy as adults to stop appreciating the wonder of a child when we are faced with the many practical situations of caring for them. As parents, teachers or caregivers, we may unintentionally try to live their lives for them. We may become overprotective in order to shield them from pain, restrict their freedom because we have our own reputations to protect, or even abandon them emotionally to deal with our own problems. As a result of overprotectedness, fear or abandonment, children may lose their sense of self and develop a low self-esteem. When this occurs, they begin to act out, and may be seen as the "problem" in the family.

The traditional solution to these problems has been to create more rules and more severe punishments, rather than to probe the message of the child's dysfunctional behaviour. Even in the problems they present, children are a gift: while it is hard for us to admit that our children may mirror our greatest fears or hopes, getting to the root of the issue will ultimately bring us peace and freedom.

The Mirror of Our Hidden Selves

Karla was hooked by her daughter's behaviour; it took her back to the pain of her own childhood experience, which she had buried in her shadow. Her daughter became a mirror of Karla's true self.

In a relationship with another person, a mannerism or behavioural pattern that disturbs us may echo something we have not resolved within ourselves. Perhaps the other person is overcritical, overbearing, controlling, or perhaps quiet, sullen, aloof. Whatever the dynamic, we intensify the problem because their "unacceptable behaviour" unconsciously hooks us back into something in our own story, and we react.

Feelings that have been repressed, buried, stuffed and disowned can be easily touched. In anger and blame, we may unconsciously visit our accumulated feelings from the past on the other person, because we have never really dealt openly and honestly with that past issue in our own lives.

The Dynamic of Projection

The dynamic of projection is subtle: we may fail to realize that someone can upset us so easily and cause us to react so strongly. The greatest gift in the phenomenon of projection is how it mirrors our shadow personality. The other person mirrors back to us something we cannot accept; that disturbs us because, unknown to us, the same dynamic is buried within our shadow. The other person, the mirror, becomes the object of all the anger and hurt we have harboured within ourselves. We unconsciously project these feelings onto the other person.

In Karla's story, Paula's phone call about Judy's drug use was a perfect mirror of Karla's own childhood experience. The panic and the strong reaction that resulted from the phone call were unrelated to the present incident; they had their roots in Karla's early childhood.

A buried memory may also be awakened by a situation similar to the original trauma; even another person may awaken those dormant feelings. Rather than being a projection, this is a "transference." The other person may simply have some characteristics similar to those of the person who inflicted the original pain. We unconsciously transfer all the feelings we have for a significant other in our story onto the person who awakens the painful memory.

The more this happens to us, the more that pent-up feeling of hurt or anger rises within our psyche and ultimately explodes like a volcanic eruption on the unsuspecting person who triggered the response. In psychological terms, this is called an "invasion." Our conscious awareness becomes flooded with the feelings from all these repressed memories, even though they are unrelated to the present incident.

By definition, a projection or a transference can work only when the original incident and all the accompanying feelings are still repressed within the shadow. Once Karla became cognitively aware of the shadow image of the childhood incident in the kitchen, it was no longer unconscious, so she could begin to deal with it as a mature person who was in touch with the hidden roots of her pain.

Principles for Living

Two sets of guidelines, which I call the "Principles for Living" or "OFF Principles" and "Interpersonal Relationship Skills," are needed to create a healing atmosphere. When dealing with a couple, I indicate in summary form beneath the problem, which I depict in the centre of the chart, the tools and guidelines people must use to facilitate problem-solving.

OFF Principles

> NO: Judging
> Analyzing
> Criticizing
> Advising
> Fixing
> Saving
> Rescuing;
> Simply accept the other person
> unconditionally

The OFF (Our Focus is Feelings) Principles quickly restore peace and sanity to a turbulent atmosphere. They are an effective tool for interpersonal relationships, because they establish the basis of good communication. They can be used to guide both parties to accept and own their feelings rather than focusing on the other person. It is hard for people to comprehend how to use these guidelines if they are not consciously aware that, to some degree, they may have formed a habit of judging, analyzing, criticizing, fixing, saving or rescuing. The OFF Principles guide us to accept the other person unconditionally, as they are. We listen to them, really hear them, and are present to them.

If we are stuck "in our heads," it is easy to dwell on what the other person is thinking or doing, to judge and blame them, rather than to look at the feelings that are being awakened by their actions or words.

Once we have created the proper atmosphere using the OFF Principles, the next stage is to review the basic communication or listening skills we need when relating to another person at an intimate level. Each person is asked to listen to the other without interrupting or attempting to change the other's point of view or their behavioural pattern. This is a slow process, but a key to healing.

Interpersonal Relationship Skills

At Bountyfull we find that a lot of marital problems come from a deep level of pain that has not been addressed in the marriage relationship due to the partners' inability to be present to each other, to listen attentively, and to give meaningful feedback.

These skills are greatly needed today, particularly because people have ceased to be conscious of them in everyday life, due to the prevalence of TV, computers and the Internet. Typically, people are exhausted after a day's work and turn to a passive form of entertainment, the ever-present TV. The subtle effect of TV is to cut people off from each other and to break down interaction and communication. When people sit in front of the TV, or the computer, they can become totally involved in some vicarious experience that takes them away from the real world. This is not always a negative thing; it can be a positive form of relaxation, entertainment and education. On the other hand, TV, the computer and the Internet can become compulsive forms of escape from being present to and interacting with others at home.

This is one factor in the increasing number of marriage problems, broken families and single parents in our society. Other forms of escape from intimacy include working long hours, compulsive shopping, and exercising excessively. All of these behaviours reduce the possibility of, and the ability for, good interaction.

I prefer the term "listening skills" to "communication skills." "Communication" can imply simply talking to each other and exchanging opinions, ideas or points of view. To really hear the other person is much more difficult. To develop their listening skills, I help people learn how to be present to each other in the here and now. Being present is much more than using our ears to hear and our mouths to speak. It implies using our whole person, listening with our whole being, following both the verbal and non-verbal language that is used. Listening skills help us to know what is going on within the other person: to hear what is said in words, body language, facial expressions and other cues.

One woman said to her husband, "You only half listen to me." The husband admitted that when she is talking, he retreats into his own space, his own mind, either to rehearse what he is going to say, or to defend or refute what she is trying to tell him. In doing so, he loses contact with her.

Here are the four basic areas to consider in developing good interpersonal relationship skills:

1. body movement

2. eye contact

3. verbal and non-verbal following, and

4. "I and thou, here and now."

1. Body Movement

Communication is much broader and richer than just words. Our whole person conveys a message, a statement of who we are and what we feel. Feelings that we have tucked away in the safety of our shadow become unconsciously expressed through our bodies. Often when a person comes into a room, their very being conveys a message. "Vibes," or unconscious messages, are being emitted without the use of words.

When I work with a couple, I have them sit in swivel chairs so they can face each other, facilitating openness to each other. If one of them starts to feel vulnerable and wants to cut the other out, or to break the body vibes, all they have to do is turn their back, or put some object between them. If they have trouble looking at or sitting near the other person, it is very hard to give them any feedback.

Within families, this dynamic of running or hiding takes many forms. For example, a husband or wife may leave the room to do a household task, make phone calls, slam doors, check e-mail, watch TV, hide behind the newspaper, go for a run, or go out with friends. No words may be exchanged, but their actions speak forcefully and profoundly of hidden feeling.

There is a wealth of information in body language. People can create distance by sinking into a mood, which consists of aggression turned in on themselves. It becomes almost impossible to have a meaningful relationship when this happens. They will only emerge from a mood when something life-giving reaches beneath the depth of that self-pity and stirs the person to life again.

Another powerful coping skill is to become distant by building a wall of silence. They may not be consciously aware that they are protecting themselves or hiding their anger, but this coping skill gives them power. This is called "passive aggression." Instead of telling the other how they feel, they behave in a passive, angry way, which is very controlling.

2. *Eye Contact*

The eyes are the windows to the soul. The eyes of another person allow us to glimpse what is going on within the sanctuary of their soul. To be aware of that is a beautiful thing, because there is such richness in the messages the eyes convey. It is important to learn to read what the eyes are saying. They may show interest, excitement, joy, pain, anger or sorrow. The eyes can tell it all.

Making eye contact requires a real willingness to be open to the other person. If I'm facing you, I'm vulnerable. If we have eye contact, I am even more vulnerable, and this can make me very fearful. I may look away to protect myself from what you are trying to say. This is very effective. Now I control you.

3. *Verbal and Non-verbal Following*

Verbal language contains a lot of information in addition to the actual words. The tone, the inflection of the voice and the repetition of certain words or phrases serve as meaningful indicators of feelings buried in the unconscious. Words in themselves have power. In good communication skills, words are precious stones. We must treat them as though they were little gems that reflect in different ways as we turn them over.

There are two levels of verbal following, two aspects of the message: the words, and the feeling behind the words.

At Bountyfull, charting people's words demonstrates our interest and attention. We put no information of our own on the chart; rather, we record only their words. In this way we can say, "Those are your words on the chart. They are not mine." People are often amazed that we would even bother to record their words. One client remarked,

> I would be speaking so fast that when Monica would write the exact words I had just said, it would slow me down. It would slow my mind down enough that we could work together on a concrete event or situation and then we could move on. Otherwise, I just go off and I'm running forever. That's what I noticed about the writing.

In ordinary conversation at home, of course, it is not possible to write down each other's words. But this vital aspect of charting illustrates the importance of feedback in verbal following.

It is very easy, and so common, to respond non-verbally. In the non-verbal response I do not give anything of myself. Body language can convey attentiveness, but it does not give feedback or information. We can show that we are interested in what people are saying through our bodily presence and eye contact, but for good communication we must be willing to share what is going on inside of us. Simply to nod or say "uh-huh" is an inadequate form of communication, because although it can indicate many things – such as anger, fear, irritation or lack of interest – it does not convey to the other person if anything has really been understood. Instead of hearing the other person, we assume we already know what they are trying to say. There is no real information in non-verbal feedback, and therefore it is an incomplete form of communication.

4. "I and Thou, Here and Now"

In general conversation, and especially in a session, it is important to stay in the present, in the here and now. I use the phrase "I and thou, here and now" to explain this approach. There are two aspects of this simple directive. First, before we begin to solve a difficult issue, those involved must agree not to reach back into some past incident or recurring pattern during the session. They must relate only to the present situation. Second, they are to use personal names rather than the impersonal "you" or "she" or "he" and speak directly to that person. Using names is an important part of staying in the here and now.

Referring to the past brings accumulated feelings, which are unrelated and intense, to the conversation. Instead, I invite people to define a concrete situation in the here and now, which allows the people to own what they are feeling now and to avoid judging the other person based on past experience.

Instead of blaming the other and making them feel defensive with a comment like this:

> *"You are always angry in the morning. You start off every morning fighting. It's very upsetting,"*

people must own their own feelings, and say how the other's actions make them feel, like this:

"When you shouted at me to hurry this morning, I felt upset and afraid."

See how this second statement specifies what happened, when it happened, and how the person experienced it. One person has owned her feelings around a particular incident in the here and now, which challenges her partner to hear her and to identify his feelings. Together, they can begin to deal with it. This may be difficult, for both of them may feel vulnerable in some way.

Statements such as "He did this…" or "She always does that…" or "You do that when you are worried…" or "You do that if you are afraid…" make a session impersonal and hypothetical. It is no longer "I and thou, here and now." When this happens, I

- remind people to use each other's name, and

- ask the speaker what they can own in what they are saying.

The Delicate Bond of Interpersonal Relationships

With the insights we have gained into the psychological makeup of human beings, and with the help of the "toy man" diagram, we now have a better understanding of the delicate bond that forms in interpersonal relationships. We have gained some awareness of how we operate, how we take in information, and how we constellate or organize feelings in a conscious way. The little toy man helps us to see something of the wonder and beauty of another person. We treasure that new-found relationship in a new way and commit ourselves to developing intimacy. As we appreciate the gift of that other person, we respond with all the intensity and richness of our emotions and our appetites, which bring such energy and passion to our relationship. This is the basis of a lasting bond forged in love.

As beautiful as this bond may be, it is also extremely delicate and fragile. When two people become one in mind, heart and affection, the road is not always smooth. The stress of children, financial pressures or infidelity to the union can lead to arguments and even violence.

It is difficult to get to the root of marital problems because they involve interpersonal relationships. Each person may be unaware of the hidden roots of their own brokenness, which makes it hard for them to relate to the other in a healthy way.

For this reason, each must own his or her own story and avoid blaming or reacting to the other person. Another person's problems always seem obvious, yet we may be blind to our own. We see the speck in their eye, rather than the log in our own; as a result, we may focus on changing or fixing the other person instead of ourselves. When we force our opinion and approach on the other, our efforts are doomed to fail because no one can change another person.

Discovering the Root Problems in Relationships

When people bring their marriage problems to Bountyfull, they are usually dealing with a dominant feeling, such as guilt, fear, anxiety, anger or even rage. During a session, these disturbing and intense emotions may cause one or both parties to erupt in dysfunctional behavioural patterns. Tracing the root cause of such deep emotions may be difficult because the original feeling has been buried beneath the pain. The more we harbour the hidden pain, the more the wound festers, which makes us vulnerable to anything that touches that open wound. We can deny our buried painful memories so effectively that we become aware of them only when some person or some incident unwittingly triggers them. Our buried feelings may flood our conscious awareness; those feelings then take over and dominate because of the surge of energy they possess. In psychological terms, this phenomenon of being overwhelmed or flooded by repressed feelings is called "invasion."

Let's listen to Trudy and Frank's story.

Trudy and Frank's Story: "The Cat Has Rights"

"Trudy" and "Frank" had sought professional help because they were thinking of ending their marriage. Recently Frank had reacted violently and had even thrown things at Trudy. Their counsellor was not able to help them to overcome their explosive reactions, and advised them to see a priest. He referred them to me.

They hoped they could get to the root of the problem and return peace and harmony to their home, as they did not really want to separate.

In my session with them, their buried feelings – carried by the body and expressed in body language – blocked listening and openness to each other. They had both built shells around themselves as protection from their buried pain, but acted out the pain through aggressive behaviour.

By the time I saw them, they were really on each other's case. In order to deal with their intense feelings, I saw both of them individually first to help them become aware of the source of their own problems. Although the private sessions gave them some useful insights, they found themselves slipping back into old behavioural patterns, becoming prey to the same vulnerability. Their challenge was to apply the insight from their past history to their present relationship. At the intimate level of a relationship these hidden areas of vulnerability are easily activated.

When they came together as a couple to address their inability to relate to and communicate with each other, they quickly hooked into their past pain, and their feelings intensified once more. Neither understood that an incident in their present situation had hooked them into the ghosts of their childhood pain, which was still hidden within their shadows. Their repressed feelings had been growing over the years, mushrooming, snowballing. They began the session by accusing each other, rather than referring to their feelings. Frank was less willing than Trudy was to own the insight gained in his individual session. In his anger he turned in his swivel chair and focused on me, completely cutting Trudy out.

He said, "Oh, she's done that for all these years; she's always done this." Trudy then exclaimed, "Look, he'll never change, no matter what!" If I had focused on their accelerating emotions and critical opinions of each other, they could not have resolved their differences.

Charting Marriage Problems

To set their problems in context, and to trace their current feelings to the original root in their stories, I asked Trudy and Frank to recount, in summary form, the insights they had gained in their individual sessions.

To help them comprehend the hidden dynamics in their relationship, I drew the whole picture in front of them on the flip chart. I drew both of their life stories in simple graphic symbols, using stick figures and timelines for each of them: one on the left side of the chart, and the other on the right. I depicted each family of origin, and drew little wheels underneath the houses to show how they had unconsciously dragged the past into the present.

We began to look at each story separately. Since they were open to sharing their stories, I encouraged them to recall the insight they had gained in their private sessions. It was a revelation for both of them to become aware of the root of their pain – pain that had led to the development of their disruptive coping skills. Next, I depicted the present problem in the centre of the chart. This helped them to see how the present problem had constellated their feelings.

Diagram of the house on wheels
depicts how we unconsciously carry
our hidden pain all our lives.

This picture takes them beyond surface problems in the present to the hidden roots, the hooks that awaken such intense feelings towards their spouse.

Concrete Example: The Here and Now

I challenged Trudy and Frank to recall a recent incident that had resulted in the present crisis, and to identify their feelings. They had to discover for themselves where the intense feelings came from. (Recounting a concrete situation moves people beyond their intensified emotions so they can focus on the facts.)

Frank replied, "Well, that's no problem, I'll give you one from this very morning." He proceeded to give a long explanation of what had happened that morning with their cat. "The cat," Frank concluded, "is part of the family. It has rights!" Then Trudy said, "Oh, no! This has got a history to it – a really long history." The problem, it seems, is the cat. Frank says, "Well, the cat is playful," and adds, "at least someone is happy." There is a hidden message behind his phrase "at least someone is happy." Clearly, the message from Frank via the cat is that Frank doesn't feel that he or Trudy is happy.

Next I got Trudy's point of view. "The cat has been such a problem, the only thing to do with the cat is, she's history!" says Trudy. The cat is at the heart of their problem.

I helped them see that the cat had hooked each of them, in different ways, into those buried feelings within their shadows. Frank's statement that "at least someone is happy" said to me: the cat is happy; nobody else is. I probed each aspect around the words they were using: for example, the word "rights." What rights does a pet have over the people in the house? Who runs the house?

Indirectly, Frank was saying that he was critical of the home and of Trudy, and that he wanted to take over and control the house. Frank had to acknowledge that the cat is not, as he had originally said, part of the family. The cat is, Frank realized, a family pet, but he felt strongly that it was not being justly treated. This realization took him back to his childhood, when he had "no rights in the family."

Somehow the cat also awakened distant painful feelings in Trudy's story. When Trudy sees the cat, she immediately becomes indignant and puts it outdoors. Franks wants to know, "Who put the cat out?" Trudy feels that if the cat does not go out, it will dirty up the place. That greatly upsets Trudy because she will "have to clean up the mess." And the fight is on!

To their amazement, they realized that their intensified feelings were polarized around the cat, which had awakened totally different feelings for each of them.

Following their feelings around the cat allowed them to focus and to avoid getting hooked by their emotions. Anger, fear, frustration, hurt and pain can be dealt with: these are soft feelings. Intense emotions – passion, rage, hatred – are out of reach.

HOOKS

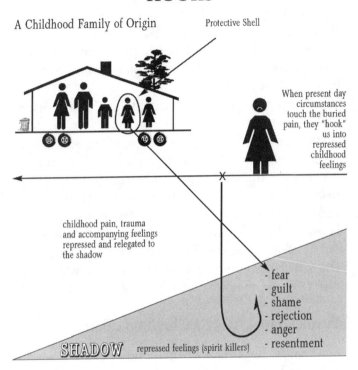

A Childhood Family of Origin

Protective Shell

When present day circumstances touch the buried pain, they "hook" us into repressed childhood feelings

childhood pain, trauma and accompanying feelings repressed and relegated to the shadow

- fear
- guilt
- shame
- rejection
- anger
- resentment

SHADOW repressed feelings (spirit killers)

The hidden feelings within our shadow can be activated by so many unconscious little incidences, or characteristics of other people, which we call 'hooks'.

In some way or another, that other person evokes the hidden memory of the original incident. These hooks dredge up from the shadow of our past story, all the repressed pain and accompanying feelings (eg. fear, guilt, anger, shame).

If we do not own these unacceptable characteristics or impulses, they tend to own us. The key is in recognizing the shadow side of ourselves, rather than repressing or living out of it. Confronting the shadow is essential for the development of self awareness.

The Symbol: The Throwaway Phrase

The cat is a perfect example of how a symbol or a throwaway phrase works. Frank says, "The cat is part of the family." He uses the cat to get the message to Trudy that not only does the cat have rights, but he has rights, too. Trudy's message is that the cat makes a mess of the house and should be kept outside.

At one point Trudy commented that "This business with the cat is utter nonsense." A judgment such as "this is utter nonsense" is a form of escape; saying something judgmental means they are "in their heads" and not in touch with their feelings. Trudy was dismissing the insight that the cat could be related to their deeper inability to communicate, but in reality, the cat did come between them. Fighting about the cat took them right out of themselves; they lost contact with the reality of the situation. Trudy saw that they were not being rational, mature adults, really present to each other.

Frank's Hook to His Childhood Pain

Frank's concern for a helpless house pet that has no rights and can't talk back recalled for him what he had learned in his private session, where he gained an awareness of how he felt as a little boy when his grandmother ran the house and he had "no rights." Before Frank was born, his father was sent to the war zone; his mother was at home, pregnant and alone, so his grandmother came to help her. All Frank knew as a child was the overbearing, angry presence of his grandmother. As early as four years of age, he yearned to know his father and be with him. Frank felt helpless without him.

Unconsciously, he developed a way of being in touch with his father by creating a war zone at home. He would disobey his grandmother and she would explode, "almost as though a cannon had gone off." And the war was on! This brought Frank much satisfaction because he felt united with his father. He would then "retreat to the trenches" and wait until calm returned.

Frank had kept all these feelings buried inside him. The cat, which he considered to be part of the family, reminded him of himself as a little boy, with no rights in his family. During the war his grandmother totally controlled the home; now he felt that Trudy was in control, while he felt powerless and angry.

Trudy's Hook to Her Painful Past

Trudy was concerned about the cleanliness of the home. The cat was continually dirtying the carpets and tearing the drapes, so she laid down the law that the cat had to be kept outside, especially when there was no one home.

Talking about her feelings towards the cat dirtying the house and how she would have to clean up after it took her back to her own childhood story.

Trudy's father was very domineering; even her mother could not stand up to him. He demanded that Trudy sit and behave properly at the dinner table. On one occasion when she made a noise eating her food, he reacted violently and threw the plate of boiled potatoes at her. They hit her in the face and then fell on the floor. He forced her to eat them off the floor, and then made her clean up the rest of the mess. She went to her room for two days and never forgave him. She felt humiliated and unjustly treated. She was powerless to do anything about it because she was a child, and her mother could not stand up for her.

The situation with the cat had awakened all those buried, hurtful childhood memories. The thought of having to clean up the cat's mess caused her to explode and vent that pent-up anger on Frank, which then sparked his volatile reaction. Frank dumped all the repressed pain of his original childhood incident on Trudy.

TRUDY

Father throws potatoes

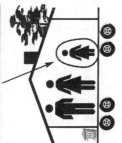

Trudy had to clean up carpet

**Trudy-
powerless, humiliated,
buried anger**

Present Problem
MARRIAGE BREAKUP

Trudy: *Cat has no rights.*
Frank: *The cat is part of the family–playful – at least someone is happy!"* The cat treated as "victim". Frank hooked into childhood pain.
Trudy: *The cat is continually dirtying the carpet and tearing the drapes.*
Trudy laid down law: **"Cat had to be kept outside!"**
Trudy refuses to clean up the carpets after the cat.
Cat hooked Trudy into her childhood pain when she was powerless, with repressed anger!

FRANK

Father, Mother, Grandmother, and Frank

Father – at war in "war zone".
Mother – pregnant.
Grandmother – overbearing, angry and violent.
Frank – "victim" no rights.

TRUDY
not part of the family.

FRANK
abandoned by father – pain of loss – repressed ANGER

Frank has succeeded in creating the "war zone" which puts him in touch with his father (*negative "pay-off"*).
The war is on!

Breakthrough

Once it became clear that the cat was the symbol that conveyed the hidden messages in Frank's and Trudy's stories, the confusion disappeared. The cat was the problem in the here and now, because it constellated all their feelings and interfered with their body language and communication, but the real problem was far deeper.

Trudy and Frank were relieved to find out that their current emotional outbursts and problems were rooted in what they had buried in their shadows: now that they had uncovered these roots, they could address the real issues.

Pent-up feelings of anger and pain have roots that are deeply buried in some long-denied painful incident. If we continually repress that anger and allow it to accumulate within our wounded soul, hidden within our shadow, it will accelerate and become magnified into an emotion of rage or excessive violence. If another person touches that buried feeling, the residue of that past hurt awakens and the pent-up feelings explode. The emotion now has its own autonomy, power and energy. We say the emotion "has us"; in other words, we are no longer in control of ourselves. We commonly use the phrase "I am beside myself." When Trudy and Frank lost control, the only means of communication they used was to act out their anger in an explosive way: to throw something, or shout, or run away.

In almost every instance, the buried root cause of anger is fear – our own or the other person's. In both instances, the protective coping skill is to explode in anger towards the other person or towards ourselves. The challenge is to identify those feelings and deal with them in the here and now, before they intensify into more harmful emotions. When a person acknowledges that they are angry and says, "I feel angry," they are able to own the root cause of their anger and can consciously deal with it.

The wealth of the insight of our buried pain and anguish, or the fear that lives shrouded within our souls, is revealed when we have the courage to find out what it is in the other person that upsets us. I ask, what are the hooks that unconsciously grasp our inner being and cause an uncontrollable reaction? These hooks are our hidden vulnerabilities that we have denied because of the pain they have caused us, the fear that they awaken within our being, or the anger that is an immediate response to touching that buried pain again. These are the spirit killers that we have examined in other chapters; we unconsciously hold on to them and harbour them within our shadow, because they have the mysterious power of hooking us into that significant other who was the cause of the original pain in our childhood or past story.

When we discover these hooks and become conscious of what is denied in our shadow, we can see how the other person is a gift to us.

In Trudy's and Frank's cases, the cat was both the problem and the gift that unlocked the buried memories of past hurts. In that way, it was a meaningful symbol in their story. As we saw in Chapter 3, a symbol can take us back to the root of the problem, while at the same time, it indicates the present difficulty and mysteriously holds the hidden message to achieve healing.

Healing Comes from Awareness

Healing comes about when people achieve a cognitive awareness of the source of the problem. When Trudy and Frank were reacting emotionally, they were not aware of the source of their hidden and buried feelings. When these were discerned, the healing process was greatly facilitated.

Our bodies and our emotions, which harbour the pain of the past, react strongly to anything that touches that previous experience. But when people are consciously aware of the root problem and have dealt with it, even if the residual pain is activated again, it no longer has the same power or control.

When their painful feelings recur, Trudy and Frank must name them and claim them – that is, bring them to a conscious awareness – and let them go. Only in this way can they take control of their lives.

In our experience at Bountyfull, this is a mature way to solve seemingly impossible situations in relationships.

Spiritual Awakening

Discovering the roots of their pain allowed Trudy and Frank to defuse their volatile feelings. Communicating as mature people can happen through patience and loving acceptance of oneself and each other. Serenity and peace depend on the degree to which each accepts and owns their new-found awareness and freedom. This awareness puts them in touch with their own spirit and they come to life. We call this "spiritual awakening."

In all these stories I hear again the echo of Christ's promise resonating throughout families: "I came that they may have life, and have it abundantly" (John 10:10).

8

Choose Life

The word is very near to you; it is in your mouth and in
your heart for you to observe. See, I have set before you
today life and prosperity, death and adversity…. Choose
life so that you and your descendants may live, loving the
LORD your God, obeying him, and holding fast to him….

(Deuteronomy 30:14-20)

When I was a child, the Bible had a special place in
our home: it was so sacred that we were taught not to
interpret it without guidance from the Church. Things
have changed since then. Now we are encouraged to
discover the treasures of God's word. The above passage
has reassured me and guided me all my life, showing me
that that hidden dynamism of the word of God goes far
beyond the written or spoken word. God himself is
within our very hearts.

In our helplessness and brokenness we often feel that
healing is far away. The above text reminds us that the
great gift of healing and the joy of finding fullness in life
are within our grasp. The word of God, addressed to all
of us, proclaims that we can share in this great mystery

of healing and be filled with the wonder of life if we but reach out in hunger for that gift.

When we probe the depths of our hidden pain and eradicate the buried roots of our problems, a lasting healing takes place within the sanctuary of our souls. This is the source of our spiritual awakening. The healing power of Christ is an energizing gift of our baptism.

The gospel tells us that the kingdom of God is within us. In the Lord's Prayer we ask God to establish this reign of love and mercy and forgiveness in our world. Our challenge is to begin within ourselves, to overcome the negativity and violence of the spirit killers in our hearts, and work towards helping to create this reign.

Cindy's Story: "I Am Alone"

"Cindy" had been through a terrible time: both her parents had been bludgeoned to death two years before, and a few months ago her sister was found murdered. Cindy had been given massive doses of medication to deaden the pain, to help her to cope and to sleep, but she was still not at peace.

As our session began, she told me that she had been depressed for the past two years, and that she thought she would never be free of the burden of grieving her family's horrific murders. She began by saying, "I am all alone. I have absolutely no family left and I fear I will be grieving all my life." To help me understand the magnitude of her grief, she placed before me, in chronological order, the graphic photos and newspaper stories of each of the murders.

The pain was still too overwhelming for her to enter into the details of the killings; she was relieved that I did not want to focus on these. My concern instead was to help her become aware of the feelings she was carrying, because feelings are always the pathways back to the deeply hidden pain. Cindy exclaimed, "My whole family is gone, I am alone and I have no will to live. Without her, life is not worth living." I realized that if she felt she could not face life without her mother, the answer to her problems lay in this obsessive relationship. Something even deeper than the murders had rendered Cindy powerless, I thought.

As we have seen in previous chapters, these hidden relational components are difficult to discern, but in them lies the answer to freedom and healing. I accepted her protestation that the trauma around the murders had almost paralyzed her. She could not let go of her grief, especially at the loss of her mother, with whom she was so close.

I drew a diagram using stick figures to help her comprehend what happens to us psychologically when we live through devastating trauma. I knew that in her heart of hearts, Cindy was willing to do anything to be freed of this intolerable grief. I showed her how, in self-protection, we build an impenetrable shell around ourselves so we can live with some internal peace. Unconsciously, we also send forceful messages to others, though we may not clearly comprehend whom we are speaking to, or what we are saying. Cindy realized that the message she was sending out was that she was a victim; she would never be free of her pain. She had shut herself off almost completely from others, obsessed with her own grief.

The drawing gave her an immediate awareness of what was happening within her. She said, "I understand what you're showing me, because I have shut down in grief ever since the murders."

When she talked about the depth of her pain at the loss of her mother, I drew the timeline of her story and her childhood home: her parents, her older sister and herself. Her father, a long-distance truck driver, was in her terms an "absentee father." For this reason she had been very close to her mother. As a child she had excelled in many different ways. She was a talented ballet dancer, a figure skater, a champion swimmer and an A student, yet she denied all this and tried to discount her accomplishments. She had even hidden her report cards to protect her older sister, who was not as gifted as she.

As she recalled her feelings throughout those years, she realized that she had always felt guilty for doing so well when her sister had done so poorly. Because her father would be outraged that her sister had not done as well, Cindy built a wall of self-denial around herself to protect her older sister.

I drew another little sketch of the home and the family, with a father in some distant country, and asked her what role she played during his absence. She said she was a close companion to her mother. Looking at the drawing, she was startled to notice that in a very real sense, she had taken her father's place and almost assumed his responsibility in the home. When we tried to discern the effect this had on her life, she became aware that unconsciously she had become a surrogate

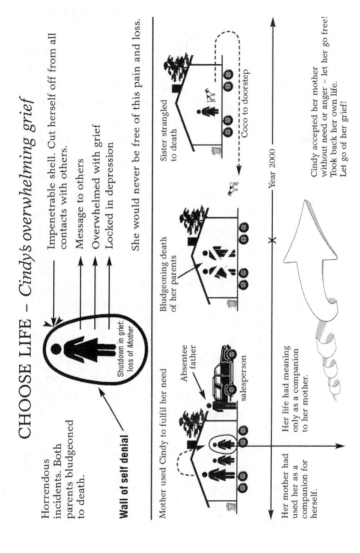

CHOOSE LIFE – *Cindy's overwhelming grief*

Horrendous incidents. Both parents bludgeoned to death.

Wall of self denial

Shutdown in grief: loss of *Mother*

Impenetrable shell. Cut herself off from all contacts with others.

Message to others
Overwhelmed with grief
Locked in depression

She would never be free of this pain and loss.

Mother used Cindy to fulfil her need

Absentee father

salesperson

Her mother had used her as a companion for herself.

Her life had meaning only as a companion to her mother.

Bludgeoning death of her parents

Sister strangled to death

Coco to doorstep

Year 2000

Cindy accepted her mother without need or anger – let her go free! Took back her own life. Let go of her grief!

175

husband to her mother. In her unconscious need for companionship, her mother had not only loved her, but used her to fill her own need.

This realization startled Cindy, because she now saw her mother in a whole new light. She had always thought that her mother was loving and protecting her, when in fact her mother had used her as a companion and had taken away her freedom to be who she really was. Cindy had always thought that her life would have no meaning unless she was a companion to her mother. This took her back to the deaths of her parents. She explained that when she received the news that they had been severely beaten, her first question was, "Is my mother still alive?" She was told that her mother had died, but her father was still struggling to hold onto life. She said that she had no feeling for her father, but was totally overcome with the loss of her mother and passed out right on the street. She felt life had no meaning.

This insight during the session gave Cindy a new awareness of what had happened to her as a child. She saw that holding onto her grief for her mother for the rest of her life would lock her into her childhood perception of her role in the home. She was amazed to discover that her grief unconsciously reduced her to being a child again, totally dependent on her mother. It was a breakthrough for Cindy to see that her grief was a coping skill that allowed her to play the victim role. At long last she was free to break the shackles of that grief, because she understood the dynamic of how it killed her own life spirit.

With this awareness, Cindy began to look at her sister's violent death by strangulation. She found that the grief she was carrying for her sister was also tied into her role of the surrogate husband. She had always taken responsibility to protect her older sister and to shelter her from pain. When she realized that she was not guilty for what had happened in her sister's life, she was able to let her sister go with peace and freedom.

In a few short hours, Cindy was able reach into her hidden pain and release the grief that had locked her into her childhood perception. In the healing, she openly faced her anger towards her mother and was able to let her go with acceptance and forgiveness. She also addressed her father and let him know how, unconsciously, she had held him responsible all her life for the pain she had felt growing up. In faith and love she turned them both over to the care and love of God, and prayed that they would rest in peace.

Finally, she took back her own life and felt that now she had the strength to move back into the family home with Cocoa, her sister's dog (see Cocoa's story in Chapter 2).

Cindy phoned recently to thank us, describing our session as "an absolutely revealing session about who I am, and where my life has taken me." Since that day she has been filled with a profound sense of peace.

The Cry of the Poor, the Voice of God

For many years now, we at Bountyfull have heard the cry of the poor and the broken as the voice of God. Rather than becoming overwhelmed or inundated by the countless revelations of people's pain and depression, I have been energized by the thrill of learning to sense that deeply hidden yet ever-present voice of God, crying out for someone to listen and respond with a caring heart. I have learned to see beyond the brokenness to help people find their spirit surging within themselves and yearning to be free. Each new person who crosses our threshold at Bountyfull is a gift and a challenge. They may be alcoholic, anorexic, bulimic, chronically depressed, sexually or emotionally broken, or addicted to drugs. They represent various faiths, races, ages and socio-economic levels. We are continually asked to broaden the vista of our experience and to develop our own life-giving gifts of sensitivity, caring and love.

In earlier chapters we have glimpsed how, in so many ways, we may lose our freedom and our joy, our spirit and our energy. We have watched with amazement as people in the stories unearthed those deeply buried roots that had taken away their life spirit. We have been filled with joy as they experienced a breakthrough, and we sensed their freedom as they took back their own lives. Vicki vowed that she would not only be free of drugs, she "would be a zombie no longer." Trudy proclaimed, "I can finally stand up to him!" The negative energy that had lived within their hearts and become spirit killers was transformed into a life-giving spirit of freedom.

The challenge for the counsellor is to pick up within the heart of a person even the slightest indications of that flickering flame of the desire to be healed. When that flame is gently fanned, the person's whole being starts to change. They begin to perceive how they can break out of that shell, and like a seed, flower into a newness of life. So often they say, "Is it really that simple?" One woman told me, "It is as though a log jam had broken, and I can now move freely." Another woman reflected, "It is like unwinding a ball of twine, strand for strand." Recently, a woman who had been terribly depressed remarked, "This is almost miraculous. I am no longer a helpless child. I am a woman and I'm free!"

Bountyfull: An Alternative Community

At Bountyfull, we have found that the solution to addictions and compulsions lies much deeper than the chemical addiction or a dysfunctional behavioural pattern. As we have seen in the stories throughout this book, we must be open to a totally new vision, which means unconditional, non-judgmental acceptance of anyone who seeks healing. Through our faith we are energized by a creative vision that challenges us to bring God's healing power, which is God's gift to us, to the tangible problems of the broken-hearted. For us, that healing lies hidden in the meaningful memories of each person.

Bountyfull is a community that is deeply rooted in the life of Christ. For this reason, our approach cannot be explained using the old categories of the traditional approach to counselling or therapy. It is a place where people who have acknowledged their grief and their powerlessness, and are searching for the peace of God, can have a breakthrough and begin to heal.

At Bountyfull we have tried to create a haven of hospitality and spirituality for people who come to us seeking healing and peace of mind. We have formed a healing community whose goals and mission statement present an alternative vision to mainstream counselling. The healing gift of God is constantly nourished within us in the breaking of the bread and Christ's resurrected presence in our lives, which we reflect on in our daily meditation on Scripture. As each of us slowly moves to an awakening of life to the full, our own personal resurrection, and to the confidence and trust that God is working within us, we are able to open up to the brokenness that comes through our doors each day. Our focus is to establish a newness in ourselves and live as a community that extends its prophetic presence to others.

Carl Jung, in writing to Bill W., the founder of Alcoholics Anonymous, clearly recommends that this kind of healing be done within a caring community. "I am strongly convinced that the evil principle prevailing in this world leads the unrecognized spiritual need into perdition, if it is not counteracted either by a real religious insight or by the protective wall of human community." (*Pass It On*, p. 384)

Each of us at Bountyfull has been challenged daily to hear the voice of God in the cry of the poor and broken. Over the years we have seen unbelievable results in people's lives; what seems like one little drop in the ocean then spreads in larger concentric circles. People's lives are changed and healed. They let go of the negative power that is controlling them and come to life. Freely, then, as they learn how to slake their spiritual thirst for union with God, they share that gift of new life with those they meet.

The subject of this book – spiritual and psychological healing of the heart – is experiential: that is why I have invited you, through real-life stories, to enter into the experiences of pain and brokenness of the people who have come to us in search of healing. Because we treasure the mystery and the gift of these stories, we ask you also to treat them with great respect.

Choose Life

The countless stories that we have been privileged to share over the years at Bountyfull House give flesh and blood to that hidden yearning for freedom in the midst of intolerable personal pain and powerlessness. The broken come through our door, one at a time, and one at a time they leave: healed, freed from the chains that bind, freed from the prisons within, free to choose life.

None of us have felt worthy of this ministry, nor do we have formal training in traditional forms of counselling. But we have each given of our own gift. We feel that we, too, have received a gift in having the daily opportunity to give of ourselves to so many people who come seeking peace, serenity and healing. The more we are in touch with who we deeply are, the more we are free to give of our own spirit, filled with the presence of God within each of us. We can be inspired by the boldness of the disciples Peter and John who, even though they were uneducated and ordinary men, exercised that healing power because they were companions of Jesus. At Bountyfull we, like Peter and John, "cannot keep from speaking about what we have seen and heard" (Acts 4:20).

All of us at Bountyfull have responded in our own way to the challenge God issues: "See, I have set before you today life and prosperity, death and adversity.... Choose life."

9

Finding Peace and Serenity in Your Life

"Let Me See Again"

As he and his disciples and a large crowd were leaving Jericho, Bartimaeus son of Timaeus, a blind beggar, was sitting by the roadside. When he heard that it was Jesus of Nazareth, he began to shout out and say, "Jesus, Son of David, have mercy on me!" Many sternly ordered him to be quiet, but he cried out even more loudly, "Son of David, have mercy on me!" Jesus stood still and said, "Call him here." And they called the blind man, saying to him, "Take heart; get up, he is calling you." So throwing off his cloak, he sprang up and came to Jesus. Then Jesus said to him, "What do you want me to do for you?" The blind man said to him, "My teacher, let me see again." Jesus said to him, "Go; your faith has made you well." Immediately he regained his sight and followed him on the way (Mark 10:46-52).

Many of us can resonate with that poignant plea of the blind man sitting alone and helpless by the roadside. He could not see; he could only feel and sense the excitement of the crowd that followed the healer. What courage it must have taken for him to shatter the silence of his darkness and confusion and cry out in those plaintive tones that still have the power to touch us deeply today: "Let me see again."

You may ask at this point, "How can I use the wealth of information in these pages to help me achieve serenity and peace in my own personal life, in my home, in my relationships with others, and in the problems I face every day? I may not feel, or be consciously aware, that I have serious addictions, or compulsions, but I do know that I face many problems and challenges in my daily life. How can I use these insights to bring me the peace and joy I so greatly desire, for myself, my family and my friends?"

At Bountyfull, the staff and many clients have observed that it takes time to grasp the concepts, to feel at ease with them, and to become aware of how they apply to our lives. Making a conscious effort to translate the simple phrases of the Serenity Prayer into our lives becomes a constant, though meaningful, task. We seldom realize that our dysfunctional behaviours have been unconscious yet clever attempts to change another person. The insights found in the "OFF Principles"(see page 148 and 188), though difficult to implement at first, can help you change your behavioural patterns. Once you have that awareness you can begin to discover your true self with openness, confidence and determination. Do not walk alone; find another person, or a group of people, with similar concerns and hopes to give you support and mirror back to you what you discern as you journey.

Where Do I Begin?

1. You begin when you realize that you have lost your peacefulness or are faced with some dilemma that you can't comprehend. The trauma or situation you are facing is the clue to your vulnerability. This is a key starting point. What gives you pain? What is the circumstance? The situation? Or, who is the person that awakens your anger or plunges you into darkness? It may be something that someone says or does, or merely a strong gut reaction to the person. Make it concrete. To recreate the dynamic of the interpersonal relationships, recall, to the best of your ability, the time, the place and the people who were present.

2. Attempt to discern what that person or situation evoked in you. What did you feel? Be free to face honestly and acknowledge your feelings without fear of the negative connotation or context in which those feelings have always been cast. Be free to name those negative feelings, be they fear, shame, guilt, anger or pain.

3. Become aware of the dynamic of the situation or incident that you lived through when those feelings arose. What happened to your relationship with the other person? What did you pick up or feel? If someone said something to you, did you feel put down, rejected, criticized, judged? What role did the other person play

in that incident? Was it someone in authority to whom you felt inferior, or was it someone you could not trust?

These relational dynamics are a gift, no matter how painful they may be, because in them you will discover that the same dynamic has been subtly present in your life in many different ways and forms, from this situation right back to the original incident, perhaps in your early childhood.

4. Attempt to discover the phrase or symbol that characterizes the interaction (for example, he or she "always makes me feel inferior, or infuriates me"). Symbols such as these may be the key to unlocking the hidden mysteries of your inner self, which you have so greatly desired to discover. They crystallize the original experience, encompass all the related feelings, and give them a unique expression.

5. With openness and freedom, follow that symbol back to discover the hidden roots buried in the experience of your early childhood. Where did you originally pick up that sense of rejection, anger, pain, guilt, shame, lack of trust or of respect?

6. Acknowledge that you have held the scars, those hidden wounds, in silence, in the depths of your being all your life. These wounds are your vulnerability. They are the hooks that in an instant can transport you back to the powerlessness of childhood, causing your life spirit and joy to vanish.

7. Discover how you coped as a child in the face of that pain. Did you learn to deny, or suppress, or run from, or escape that pain, that person, that haunting memory? Did you learn to play a game of escape or denial in order to find solace, or to meet the expectations of others? Was it a difficult learning process to develop these skills to escape, to go numb, to become arrogant, strong, hardened, or alternatively to become a perfectionist or an over-achiever in order to gain acceptance or to be compliant at any cost?

8. Realize that, in your present dilemma, your coping skills are a more sophisticated form of that early childhood game that allowed you to cope and to survive. These coping skills are not all negative. They have become part of your persona, your socially acceptable self. The negative influence they have over you comes from the unconscious power they have to transport you back to those deadening feelings in early childhood that took your spirit away.

9. Be aware that if you allow these games and these negative feelings to remain in your heart, they will become the spirit killers that take away your freedom to be who you are, the person that God has created you to be.

10. Once you have discovered who originally caused the pain, you name them and claim them for what they were in childhood. In this way you divest them of their power over you. Realize that you cannot change the past. Accept whoever the person was who caused the original

pain, and in peace set him or her free. In the process of healing, privately or in your group, you can say anything you want to the other person without harming them, because you are speaking to the shell of that early childhood perception. In so doing you learn how to slake your spiritual thirst for union with God, you set yourself free. This is the breakthrough. This is your spiritual awakening. Humbly accept that you are a gift to yourself and to the world!

Guidelines for Personal or Group Work

The OFF Principles and the Tools for Reflection

Step 1: Focus on your own person

Remember, when you are reflecting on your story, to keep the OFF Principles in mind:

NO: Judging
Analyzing
Criticizing
Advising
Fixing
Saving
Rescuing;
Simply accept the other person
unconditionally.

Stay focused on your own person, and accept yourself, first and foremost, with peace and serenity. Many of us are our own harshest critics. Discard the learned, critical, negative ways of looking at yourself;

cease to be the judge, the jury and the executioner. Don't be afraid to face the fear that may arise as you reflect on feelings that are disturbing. Don't run from them, don't hide them, don't deny them: face them for what they are – feelings – and own them.

Step 2: See your life as a story

Approach this task with freedom and a sense of adventure by seeing your life as a story, and not as an accumulation of duties, responsibilities, burdens or problems. Focus on discovering the mystery and uniqueness of the Spirit of God within the earthiness of your being. You are fearfully, wondrously made! (Psalm 139:14) Seeing your life as story allows you to thrill with the joy of the child awakening to a whole new world of discovery and to understand your story now with a deeper insight and knowledge of how it has unfolded.

Consider your life as a drama. You are writing a story and you are the central character, the hero. Let your life unfold from your early childhood with the awakening of awe and wonder, even though your early life may have been shattered by pain, rejection or violence. Reflect on how you shut down when you experienced the pain and rejection, and crawled into your shell and cut the world out. Look back on that child with care, love and understanding, and above all, acknowledge your strength and spirit to persevere through those trials and that pain. You learned to deal with intolerable difficulties and continued to develop and flower into fullness. You, the hero, survived.

Step 3: Make a chart of your story

This is a simple and playful means of doing your own journalling. In order to get a better sense of relationships, draw little stick figures and depict the hidden messages or feelings that become more evident as you begin to put them down in graphic symbols. Be concrete: recall the actual incident and, to the best of your ability, recreate the original setting in your mind. Bring the other people into the picture as though they are actors on the stage with you. Again, remember that you are looking at the whole story and trying to get a comprehensive overview of your whole life. Don't stay focused on the present pain or problem.

Step 4: Develop awareness of repeated behavioural patterns

Learn to identify and become aware of repeated behavioural patterns and familiar roles that have had a long history in your story. Roles are your position in the family. What were your responsibilities? What burdens did you carry without mentioning a word to others? Did you live in fear or anger, or did you suppress these feelings? Realize that out of your buried pain, you unconsciously sent messages to others. Were the messages actual words, or were they actions that symbolized the pain and the burden you felt, even though the other person was not aware of or sensitive to it? Were you powerless or helpless as a child? Did you become the victim or the martyr and develop the "poor me" syndrome?

Be aware that your helplessness or powerlessness is often the key to where the problem came from, and hence where the solution lies.

Step 5: Name it, claim it and let it go

Understand that your dysfunctional behaviours were the result of your childhood perception of the world around you and the people who shared your journey. These behaviours were originally your coping skills or survival techniques. The cognitive awareness of that childhood perception will set you free. It allows you to accept your story in all its fullness, to fearlessly name it and claim it without any of the residual feelings of fear, anger, guilt or shame, and to let the past go. Acknowledge the beauty of that child. Accept yourself unconditionally. In doing so, the deeply buried roots of your life spirit are re-energized and awakened. You are free to move yourself from within, to relate freely in a whole new way to your life story. You are free to own all the gifts that have been yours throughout your life, from the unfathomable gift of your unique being and your ability to relate to God, to the gift of others and the beauty of creation that surrounds you.

Step 6: Find a supportive community

In doing this work, don't isolate yourself from other people and work only introspectively. If you can, become part of a supportive community or group of people, such as a 12-Step group, who are searching for the same peace and serenity and are anxious to apply these new-found principles and directions in their lives. Learn to be open.

* * * * *

God speaks to each of us in so many ways, and especially in the baffling negativity of our brokenness and pain. With God's help, and with your friends and guides along the way, you can find freedom and healing in your life.

May this be a joyful, life-giving experience for you, and may you learn to cherish the unique gift that you are. Small though you may be, you are God's gift to our world. I wish you the fullness of God's blessings.

Appendix:
Prophetic Insights
for the Counsellor

In attempting to help people achieve that release from the prison of past hurts and the present compulsion to addictions and destructive behavioural patterns, I was inspired by Isaiah:

> Here is my servant, whom I uphold,
> my chosen, in whom my soul delights;
> I have put my spirit upon him;
> he will bring forth justice to the nations.
> He will not cry or lift up his voice,
> or make it heard in the street;
> a bruised reed he will not break,
> and a dimly burning wick he will not quench.
>
> *(Isaiah 42:1-3)*

These prophetic words spoke directly of the coming of Christ and his compassionate mission of healing for our broken world. As we follow in the footsteps of Christ today, they are meaningful guidelines for all of us as we strive to hear the voice of God in the cry of the poor and the broken.

Here, in summary, are six key guidelines for counsellors.

1: *Be Totally Present*

Counsellors must be totally present to others in a session, so they will feel that someone is really listening to their story. At Bountyfull we begin with the present concern or pain and slowly help them rise above it as they see where it has come from in their story. It is very difficult for people to present their whole life story in its brokenness and pain to another person. As counsellors we help the person whose heart is broken and whose life is unmanageable to accept themselves as they become aware of how their story unfolded – a delicate process.

2: *Use OFF Principles*

Over the years I have transposed the prophetic words of Isaiah 42, quoted above, into what we call the "OFF Principles." OFF stands for "Our Focus is Feelings"; these principles have become touchstones of Bountyfull House:

NO: Judging
Analyzing
Criticizing
Advising
Fixing
Saving
Rescuing;
Simply accept the other person
    unconditionally.

People tend to judge, criticize and condemn others. At Bountyfull we try to take people "out of their heads" and allow them to focus on their feelings. Feelings have been given poor press and have been denied for too long. Yet they are the value quotients of our lives; they give tone, quality and colour. They help us to discover who we are. Feelings are very difficult to discern if they are squelched by our intellect. Those skills are the ones that we put on hold in the OFF Principles. We focus on feelings and do not judge, analyze, criticize, advise, fix, save or rescue.

As counsellors, we must have no preconceived judgment about the client's story. We must be open to whatever arises as we listen to them. Although many of the actions described are morally and legally problematic, it is not our role to judge or punish.

After all, people who are in profound pain and are driven by some unconscious compulsion are not acting rationally and therefore are not morally responsible for their actions, although they are legally responsible. Also, there is a world of difference between being guilty for an act committed with full intent of the will, and feeling guilty for something that happened in childhood.

The role of the counsellor in the healing process is to help people understand their dysfunctional behaviour in its proper context. As I work with a person, I keep this awareness before me. This allows me to accept the person totally and non-judgmentally, in the hope that they can discover how their actions have become the expression of a broken heart. I recall St. Paul's admonition in his second letter to the Corinthians: "Our competence is from God, who made us competent to be ministers of a new covenant, not of letter but of spirit; for the letter kills, but the Spirit gives life." (2 Corinthians 3:5-6)

People often slip back into the shell of imprisonment because it is the comfortable negativity in which they have lived their lives. During a session, as they follow their story, they may become like children again. They lose control emotionally and are overcome with grief and sadness. Sometimes they even begin to look like a child. They may slouch in the chair and seem to give up; curl up in the chair or fall defiantly silent, as if to say, "You cannot break through this wall." As long as they remain locked within the prison of their childhood perceptions, they will remain immature children. If we, as counsellors, are disturbed by their behaviour, we allow them to stay in that childhood role of victim. By remaining focused and not reacting to the childlike game they may be playing, we draw them out of that protective shell, that role of victim, without saying a word.

When the counsellor accepts people unconditionally, this generates a feeling of trust, which puts them at ease.

3: Discovering the Past

Slowly and with probing questions, with no input of suggestive or directive information, I help people to recreate their story. Using a 3- x 5-foot flip chart, I chart their whole life story on a timeline in front of them as they begin to trace the painful memories of the past. I begin where they are in the current situation or trauma, then follow back the pathway of their story, indicating these incidents on the timeline. I always start with what they are feeling and allow them to define the concern that they presently carry.

I assist them to revisit their early memories and, in their imagination, to see themselves once more in the home of their childhood. Stick figures representing their parents and siblings and a little sketch of their home on the flip chart encourage the memories to flow. There is a certain detachment in viewing the sketch, almost as though they are seeing someone else's story. This allows great freedom and often evokes memories that have long been buried and denied in fear.

It is amazing to watch someone move through the many emotions evoked by these simple stick figures and the interconnecting lines that are used to depict the numinous interpersonal relationships that still carry memories – memories that may still carry charged and emotionally explosive feelings.

4: Discern the "Gift" of Our Pain – Craving Wholeness

In our work at Bountyfull, we have a deep respect for the dignity of those who humbly come to us seeking peace and serenity. We know that beneath the brokenness of destructive behavioural patterns lies a heart craving freedom and wholeness. I realize, too, that their pain holds the mystery of their healing, because it comes from the very root of their brokenness. In that way, and that way only, pain is a great gift to us. But we must learn to face it and enter into it, rather than deny it, run from it, or numb it with medication, chemical addictions or behavioural compulsions. If we face it, it can guide us to freedom. For beneath that buried pain is the deeper and more meaningful constant craving for wholeness, that yearning to be connected to the core of our being and to be free to live life to the full.

5: Accept the Past

How can people possibly make peace with a troubled past? The key is acceptance. At Bountyfull, we do not focus primarily on forgiveness, but on acceptance. The power of acceptance completely changes the whole tone and deepens people's awareness of the original incidents in their stories.

The well-known "Serenity Prayer" that is part of the AA program gives clear directions in this regard, even if people are not consciously aware of what they are saying when they recite it:

> God grant me the serenity
> to accept the things I cannot change,
> the courage to change the things I can,
> and the wisdom to know the difference.

When people accept past failings as things they cannot change, however horrendous they may seem, and they openly and honestly face and accept them simply as facts, they find a quiet sense of release and relief. They stop living in denial. They become free to relate their life stories with care and compassion, acknowledging difficulties and childhood traumas that were part of their journey. Then they are free to look at their story in a mature and rational way, to "name it, claim it and let it go." It is simply their story. Acceptance is the primary stage of forgiveness, preceding movement into any form of healing.

6: *Cognitive Awareness*

People can see pain as a gift only if they have a cognitive awareness or understanding of how their search for freedom and independence developed into dysfunctional behavioural patterns, which are unconscious symbols and expressions of the pain that has been buried so deeply in their story. This pain has become the driving compulsion behind their addictive behaviours, which are both the present problem and an indication of the hidden pain. When they become consciously aware of what or whom they have been holding onto, they will have a clear insight into the direction for healing. Then they can consciously let go of the pain that is the root cause of their suffering.

Counsellors must be caring and cautious as they begin to break through that shell and open the "graves" in which the spirit has been entombed.

> "You shall know that I am the LORD, when I open your graves,
> and bring you up from your graves, O my people. I will put
> my spirit within you, and you shall live, and I will place you on
> your own soil; then you shall know that I, the LORD, have spoken
> and will act – says the LORD."
>
> *(Ezekiel 37:13-14)*

Pitfalls for the Counsellor

It is very important for the counsellor not to react, either to individuals or to their stories. We must be very careful not to get caught, or "hooked," by whatever they tell us. When we are following a client's story for a period of two to three hours, we encounter endless emotions that may hook us into our own stories. We may be subtly moved by compassion, caring or empathy for the other person; we may be overwhelmed by another's pain, especially when it touches our own hidden pain. It is easy to identify with the child in a client's story if the counsellor identifies with the hurting child in himself or herself.

The following case shows how one of our counsellors unconsciously became hooked while listening to a client's story.

Joanna's Story: "Stuffing Down Feelings"

"Joanna" was pretty and petite, with blonde hair framing her face. She looked much younger than her 36 years. Mid-session Joanna exclaimed tearfully, "This is a *real problem*. It's an addiction. I'll go home and just eat and eat until I can't *move*! It's like an addiction, like I'm addicted to drugs or something!"

Joanna had recounted a painful incident that occurred when she was eight years old. She had disobeyed her mother and made a mess by spilling some paint. As a result, her mother punished her and Joanna was not "included" in the family meals for several days afterward. From that day forward, her mother never again made a school lunch for Joanna. She felt this was "harsh" treatment; what she learned from it was that if she did something wrong, if she made a mistake, her basic need – food – would not be met.

As Kathy walked through her story with Joanna, she noted her dynamic words and feelings on the flip chart. Joanna used the words "harsh," "not included," "isolated" when describing the incident around the spilled paint. She later used the same words to describe an incident at work. The presence of the words on the chart made a clear connection between her childhood pain and her present struggles. Joanna recognized the fear and confusion she experienced as a child of having food taken away when she "did something wrong." When circumstances in her adult life triggered those same feelings, she saw how she used a coping skill she had learned in childhood: she ate until she couldn't eat any more, because the food might be taken away.

This took Joanna back to a time when her family moved into a "little shack in the woods," with "no heat, water, electricity or phone." Joanna hid the fact of where she lived from the other children at school, for fear they would make fun of her, and not "include" her. She mentioned again how isolated and unhappy she was in this little shack in the woods. She recalled how her father would bring home the groceries and she and her sister would "leap on the food." Joanna would "eat as much as I possibly could, until I couldn't eat any more. All the

Appendix

sweets would go then, because there might not be any more later." She became withdrawn and shy and felt very "isolated" in the new environment.

Her dad was a quiet workaholic who spent long hours at work; when he was at home, he mostly slept. Her mom, on the other hand, was a stay-at-home mom whom Joanna described as angry, domineering and judgmental (although she was quick to add that her mother always greeted her and her sister with a smile and spent much time talking with them about their day after school).

Joanna recognized how, unconsciously, throughout her adult life she had been "holding onto her mother." She saw that she was using food to send a message to a significant other – her mother – or to hold on to her mother as someone her childhood perception was telling her she needed. She had never been aware that her eating was a message to her mother that "I am in control." When Joanna discovered the root of the pain in her story and what food was for her, what it did for her, who it put her in touch with, she become consciously aware of what was driving her compulsion to eat. With food she "stuffed down" all the feelings she was too afraid to own. Discovering the root of the painful feelings that triggered old coping skills brought Joanna awareness and peace. Healing came as she let go of her parents with love, and saw food for what it was meant to be in the first place: nourishment for her body. She took back her power, her sense of self. And that was a gift for her.

The Hook

As Kathy and I reviewed Joanna's story, Kathy said she was disturbed by Joanna's comments about overeating and her statement "This is a *real problem*. It's an addiction...like I'm addicted to drugs or something!" Kathy was aware of the dynamic that took place when Joanna learned her coping skill. She realized that Joanna's connection with her dad, the feelings of isolation and fear, and the coping skill of overeating, all hooked her into her own story. She reflected that she could feel the connection between "Dad not being there" and Joanna's response to her dad coming home, bringing the food, and eating all she possibly could. She recalled especially how she had become distracted and felt a "vague discomfort" with Joanna's phrase "eating as much as I possibly could, until I couldn't eat any more." At this point Kathy reflected, "In my own mind I wondered if she was being abused, as I was when my dad came home. Overeating had been my coping skill to numb the pain my of abuse."

It was then that Kathy saw how she was hooked by Joanna's story. The thought that Joanna may have been abused was from Kathy's story, not Joanna's. Once Kathy knew what had happened, she became consciously aware of the hook. She let it go, and once more became present to Joanna and her pain.

Later Kathy reflected, "I got hooked, and rediscovered a ghost in my own shadow. It didn't kill me; I'm stronger than before. A gift!"

Healing by Personal Discovery

As we can see in the above stories, self-discovery is the key to the healing process. The counsellor must not contribute any information to the session, but rather follow the feelings and the actual phrases of the client. All the words written on the chart must be the words of the client.

If the counsellor makes any assumptions, or begins looking for symptoms, he or she may move away from what the client is actually experiencing. Assumption on the counsellor's part may result in leading the client in a false direction. Unconsciously, the counsellor may begin to make a mental character sketch of the client, and presume to know more about the client than the client himself or herself knows.

Counsellors must be very careful not to evoke what is called "false memory syndrome." For instance, when a counsellor thinks that a person is burying a memory, such as an incident of abuse, it is possible to lead the person into a false memory. Once I had a client who was having a very hard time with the information that had come up with another counsellor. He had been instructed that his was a typical sexual abuse situation, when in reality this was not true. There is a great temptation to see sexual abuse as the bottom line in many cases. Even in cases where there has been sexual abuse, it may not be the ultimate cause of the problem that is disturbing the person now. Sometimes the most devastating pain in such cases is not caused by the abuser, but by the absence of the loving care of someone who should have been there for the child. For this reason it is extremely important to establish concrete situations in stories, and avoid making any hasty assumptions.

We do not "classify" people as a certain "type" according to what other theories may say. Labelling or categorizing can inhibit their freedom to contact the painful memory.

Rather than allowing clients to get into any theories, what I call "head trips," I simply ask people to be in touch with what their heart has experienced. There is no way we can directly access the unconscious. Jung, in his treatment of the endopsychic functions of the psyche, indicated that we can only "postulate," or evoke, what is buried in our shadow by searching through the memories of our past experiences. When people recount a troubling experience in their present life using a concrete example, the feelings surrounding the incident may evoke a memory of an earlier experience, including all the pain around it. In this way, what has been repressed will surface. It is extremely important that they describe a real experience, because it holds the key to how their body was influenced in that situation. We must help them learn to read the messages that have become the expression of that hidden pain.

The concrete experience has the subtle effect of challenging the person to "get out of their head"; that is, to stop trying to analyze the situation for themselves. They then begin to focus with more peacefulness, recreating the memory of what really happened, and can discern the messages that the defensive behavioural pattern has conveyed.

Repressed fear can be released only when people discover who has held the key to denial, who is their jailer. Who committed them to a prison of pain for life? Who was the cunning, caring one to whom they relinquished their freedom in order to gain love or attention? In Rose's case, her mother and aunt were her jailers. These deeply hidden secrets can be awakened only if we are gentle enough to sense the movements, however slight, of a broken heart, and to read the language of survival in the journey through the years.

People must discover for themselves how they have lost their life-giving spirit. The counsellor must resist the temptation to tell them how to change or behave. As we follow a life story, retracing the pathway of the repressed pain that has been denied and buried in their shadow, people slowly begin to nurture that flickering flame of the life spirit that is imprisoned within them. We believe that the person must have an "aha!" experience of how their buried pain has been the hidden source of their destructive behaviour. They then become free to reclaim their lost power.

Charting the Life Story

As I said earlier, at Bountyfull we chart each person's life story on a 3- x 5-foot flip chart, showing key incidents and relationships by drawing a timeline and stick figures.

When people refer to home or family members, I draw simple diagrams or symbols of these. This allows them to move in a direction that is right for them, and stops me from leading the session. Thinking about family members helps people move back into that distant setting with ease. Memories are evoked and relationships are recalled, where before there had been nothing but a blank and a simple protestation of "I don't know" or "I can't remember anything from way back there."

Charting their story on flip chart also allows them to observe their own story more objectively as it unfolds, and frees them of guilt and fear they have carried. Visualizing something so personal almost instantly brings peace and relief, because they can view it with detachment and then experience the thrill of discovery for themselves.

Principles in Charting

We use the following principles in charting:

1. *Indicate on the right on the timeline the present trauma that the person is dealing with.*

2. *Focus on feelings and coping skills, not on any intellectual insights that emerge.*

We strive to keep people out of their heads and in touch with their feelings. On the left side of the chart, beneath the timeline, we record in their own words the feelings and the coping skills that surround a particular experience.

3. *Continually challenge the person to give concrete examples from their life story.*

Recalling concrete experiences leads people away from expressing opinions and analyzing. The concrete examples they provide often evoke old memories of long-forgotten incidents. I ask clients to try to remember as many specifics as they can: the time of day or night, where the event took place, who was there.

4. *Record the dysfunctional behavioural patterns, dynamic feeling-toned phrases and symbols that are charged with energy and power and speak of the pain buried in the root experience.*

The dysfunctional behavioural patterns that have resulted from buried pain are the signposts along the paths that we retrace to the early childhood experience. These are our focus, for they lead us to the root of the problem. The root not only gives us all the dynamics we need to understand what has caused the loss of sense of self, it also reveals who the significant other is and what killed the person's spirit.

5. *Be aware that the confusing messages of the dysfunctional behavioural patterns give tangible expression to the compensatory relationship between the unconscious and the conscious.*

Dysfunctional behavioural patterns are expressions of buried pain that symbolize and make visible, in that childhood "foreign language," the yearning for healing that indicates

- the source of the problem

- the present frustration, and

- how to bring about healing.

6. *Help people become cognitively aware that the treasure of their lost sense of self lies buried beneath all the accumulated guilt and pain within their broken hearts.*

What does the broken spirit want to convey to the conscious awareness? Behavioural patterns, however bizarre or distorted they may seem, speak of a spirit yearning to be free. The goal is for the person to discover that hidden message in a conscious way in order to restore their lost sense of self, be filled with a new energy and become united to the root of their being. Their life spirit awakens to a sense of freedom and love of self and others. This is the treasure that prompted the man in the parable to go out and buy the whole field. May that be God's gift to you.

Glossary

affective abilities: those bodily powers that add a feeling quotient to the object of our senses (such as desire and passion)

affective feeling-toned phrase: describes feelings that cause a physiological enervation that affects our bodies

brokenness: the result of a heart broken by some intolerable buried pain

complex: a fixed organization of psychic facts within our ego

constellations: fixed patterns that we form through repetition to organize information brought in from the external world

dynamic feeling-toned phrase: a phrase that combines a feeling that determines the value quotient and describes the intensity of the energy that it contains

dynamism: conveys an inherent energizing force

ego: the faculty that organizes the psychic facts within our conscious awareness *endopsychic functions*: a system of relationships between the contents of the consciousness and postulated processes in the unconscious. There are four functions: 1. memory; 2. feelings; 3. emotions; 4. invasion.

foreign lands: denotes a psychological state of mind in which we unconsciously live, within unrelated memories of past experiences buried in our shadow rather than being in touch with the reality of our present situation

inferiority complex: feelings that have been constellated to perceive ourselves as "less than"

intimate sanctuary: used to indicate a sacred space within ourselves

invasion: the fourth of the Jungian endopsychic functions, which depicts the psychological phenomena of the conscious awareness being overwhelmed by the intrusion of buried psychic facts

land: a term used to denote the "homeland" within our real selves in which we harbour our true sense of self buried within our psyche

negative payoff: the unconscious psychological game we play whereby we hold onto negative or repressed painful memories in order to unconsciously connect with some significant other in our lives

numinous: a spiritual, intangible relational reality within our psyche

persona: our socially acceptable self or mask that we wear to hide our buried pain; it can become an unconscious part of our personality *projection*: the psychological function that attributes to another individual the buried contents or attitudes hidden within our own personal unconscious or shadow

receptive powers: the psychological functions that allow us to contact external facts given to us by our senses

spirit killers: the psychological results of repressed facts that we retain within our psyche; the denied, painful feelings that diminish or completely divest us of our energy and our sense of self

symbols: a word, phrase, action or object that characterizes or gives a unique expression to some hidden message; an external sign of an unconscious reality

throwaway phrase: a casual phrase that is often repeated and treated as a meaningless and offhand expression, but actually conveys a deep, hidden message that can be discerned in the fact of its constant repetition

transference: the psychological function that attributes to another individual characteristics and attitudes repressed within our own shadow that refer to someone in our past experience (Jung, *Analytical Psychology*, 1968, p. 15)

victim complex: a constellation of negative experiences that we retain in our ego and that unconsciously becomes a fixed way of perceiving ourselves as a victim

waking dream: describes the unconscious state in which a person lives, in a fantasy-like world in which they live out the symbol of their repressed pain